Arduino Projects

Herb Norbom

Where we are aware of a trademark that name has been printed with a Capital Letter. Great care has been taken to provide accurate information, by both the author and the publisher. No expressed or implied warranty of any kind is given. No liability is assumed for any damages in connection with any information provided.

Table of Contents

PREFACE

The purpose of this book is to provide more advanced projects to the Arduino user. We will not go into the details of installing software. The user should have a basic understanding of the Arduino IDE. Multiple versions of the Arduino IDE were used in the sketches, versions 1.8.8, 1.8.9 and 1.8.10, older versions will probably work as well. The book will be most useful to the users that have developed some applications for the Arduino using the built in IDE. The projects were completed on a Windows10 PC with the Arduino Uno and Nano. While not tested the projects shown will probably work on Linux and OS platforms with some changes as well as on other Arduino development boards.

This book includes the <u>printed</u> source code and wiring diagrams for the projects. The electronic or digitized source code is available to download for an additional fee and for a limited time. The download includes the digitized program source code and color PDF circuits. A limited time Discount is available. The Discount code is listed later in this book along with the web site.

FORWARD

The Arduino is an open-source platform with relatively easy to use hardware and software. The software that makes this system easy to use is the Arduino programming language. This software takes the C and C++ languages to a higher level. This largely eliminates the need for the user to become involved with programming at the bit level. Appropriate microchip registers are set as needed by the various software libraries. "The Arduino was born at the Ivrea Interaction Design Institute as an easy tool for fast prototyping, aimed at students without a background in electronics and programming...All Arduino boards are completely open-source..."[1]

The reader will expand on the programs included by adding new features and combining the various programs into their projects.

We have not included sources for the products used in the examples. The Arduino and the products used are widely available. An internet search will reveal many sources and price variations. We do recommend Adafruit and Sparkfun as sources due to their tutorial's and software. Most of the projects are shown using the Uno but the Nano and other Arduino development boards will also work with appropriate changes.

---

[1] **Arduino web page** https://www.arduino.cc/en/guide/introduction

Project First used on	Part Description
1	Arduino Uno with USB Cable (some projects require two) or two Nano's
1	Nano with USB Cable (some projects require two) or two Uno's
1	Half size breadboard two required for some projects (recommended but full size will also work).
2	Wall Adapter Power Supply (Optional)
2	Wire you can cut multiple colors would be good, suitable for breadboard (optional)
2	Premium Male/Male Jumper Wires – 20 x6"
2	Premium Male/Female Jumper Wires – 20 x6"
2	Trimpot 10K with Knob (Potentiometer)
2	LED (this is for red 25 pack)
2	Resistor 220Ω at least two, but suggest a Resistor Kit prices vary by kit
4	Tactile Button switch (6mm) x 20 pack
5	DHT11 basic temperature-humidity sensor
5	Photocell (CdS photoresistor)
5	Resistor 10kΩ, may come with temperature-humidity sensor
6	Small low voltage and amperage fan or use small motor
6	H-Bridge SN754410 Quadruple Half
7	Soil Moisture Sensor (usually a pack of 5)
7	small hobby pump, low voltage low amperage
8	LCD compatible with Hitachi HD44780 driver
9	Ultra-Sonic Sensor HC-SR04
9	Resistor 1.2kΩ
10	RGB Color Sensor White LED TCS34725 (requires soldering)
11	OLED I2c IIC Serial LED LCD Screen Display Module for Arduino
12	D Card suggest minimum 8Gb
12	Micro SD Card Adapter Reader SPI Interface
16	Speaker low voltage and amperage with built in amplifier
17	Analog Thumb Joystick, two potentiometers

Project First used on	Part Description
18	Hobby Gearmotor -200 RPM(Pair) We like these as leads are already soldered (But ROB-13258 work)
18	Wheels -65mm (Rubber Tire, Pair)
18	Battery Pack for Arduino (Optional) Many sources check specs to ensure correct voltage and mAh. I like ones that have on/off switch. Suggest 9.6V 2000mAh
19	Vishay Infrared Receiver TSOP32338SS1V
19	Remote Infrared Transmitter, Roku used in example, but any should work
19	Arduino Nano with USB Cable for some projects
19	Infrared Obstacle Avoidance Sensor **NEED 2** of these for project
20	Sharp Infrared Distance Sensor 2Y0A02
21	Tower Pro SG92 Micro Servo
22	two -FEETECH FSR90R 360° Rotation Continuous Servo with wheels
23	Sensor Shield or Expansion board for Nano v5.0
25	Stepper 28BYJ-48 with Driver Board ULB2003
26	Stepper 4 Bipolar wire using H-Bridge, STH-390254 1.8Deg-Step 60Ω
28	MPU6050 6 Axis Gyro Accelerometer Module (may require soldering)
29	Bluetooth HC-06
29	Nano Expansion Adapter Breakout Board IO Shield for Arduino, two needed if using Nano's
30	RFM69 HCW two needed
30	Logic Converter 5V to 3V (Two needed)
30	Capacitors suggest a kit of various sizes

Project 1: Simple Calculator Arduino

This is a simple program or script to familiarize you with the Arduino Serial Monitor and some math operations. You will also use some of the built-in functions for converting 'string' input to 'float' values. The program computes the results for addition, subtraction, multiplication, division, square root and exponential powers.

Attach the Uno to your computer with the USB connector. In the IDE click on TOOLS and check that correct BOARD and COM port are selected. I am using Arduino IDE and have noticed that for the PROCESSOR I need to select the (old bootloader). IF YOU ARE GETTING errors such as shown in the following the processor maybe incorrect. Try selecting "old bootloader".

Enter the following code and upload the sketch to the Arduino.

/* **Arduino_simpleCalculator for Arduino Uno or Nano Herb Norbom 3/31/2019**
 accepts float input up to two decimal points

 for subtraction precede number with minus sign

 for multiplication precede number by *

 for division precede number by /

 for square root enter 's' for square root of result

 for power of enter 'p' followed power integer

*/

```
float result = 0.0;
char inChar ="";
int inputLength = 0;
String inputString="";
boolean stringComplete = false;

void setup() {
  Serial.begin(9600);
  Serial.println("Enter number ");
}

void loop() {
  if (stringComplete){
    if (inputString[0] == 'c'){ //Note you must use single quote vs dual
      Serial.println("clear total");
      result = 0.0;
    }
    else if (inputString[0] == '/'){ //Note you must use single quote vs dual
      Serial.print("divide by input of: ");
      inputString.remove(0,1);
      Serial.println(inputString);
      result = result / inputString.toFloat();
    }
```

```
  else if (inputString[0] == '*'){ //Note you must use single quote vs dual
    Serial.print("multiply by input of: ");
    inputString.remove(0,1);
    Serial.println(inputString);
    result = result * inputString.toFloat();
  }
  else if (inputString[0] == 's'){ //Note you must use single quote vs dual
    Serial.print("square root of: ");
    Serial.println(result);
    result = sqrt(result);
  }
  else if (inputString[0] == 'p'){ //Note you must use single quote vs dual
    Serial.print("integer power of result by: ");
    inputString.remove(0,1);
    Serial.println(inputString);
    result = pow(result,inputString.toInt());
  }
  else {
    Serial.print("add to result using input of: ");
    Serial.println(inputString);
    result = result + inputString.toFloat();
  }
 Serial.print("Result: ");
 Serial.println(result);
 stringComplete = false;
 inputString="";
 }
}
void serialEvent() {
 while (Serial.available()) {
  char inChar = (char)Serial.read();
  inputString += inChar;
  if (inChar == '\n') {
    stringComplete = true;
  }
 }
}
```

The settings for the serial monitor are show in the example. Make sure the baud rate and Newline are as shown in the example.

Project 2: Potentiometer

This project does not need the Arduino. You do need a low voltage supply, I suggest 3.3V if not using the Arduino. No programing. Just to get you familiar with breadboard and Arduino pin out. The resistor is to help prevent LED burnout. If using the Arduino use the 3.3V to power the breadboard. With the potentiometer the center pin is generally for output. Use a wire from the center pin to the leg of the LED. If the LED will not light be sure you have not reversed the anode and cathode. The longer leg of the LED is the anode or positive leg. Use a 220Ω resistor to help prevent LED burnout.

Project 3 Potentiometer Voltage

Expanding on our previous project we are using the Arduino and the analog pin to calculate voltage. We will use the 5V power source from the Arduino. **Do not use an external power source**. The analog reading and related voltage are displayed on the serial monitor, you can also use the serial plotter.

```
/*Arduino_Measure_Voltage 4/18/2019 Herb Norbom
  Displays raw analog measurement and associated voltage
  If using 3.3 v  raw values will be 0 to 691
  If using 5.0 v  raw values will be 0 to 1023
  Use a multimeter to get actual voltage the Arduino outputs.
*/


int PinA0 = A0;    // select the input pin for the potentiometer
int readingA0 = 0;  // variable to store the value coming from the sensor

void setup() {
  Serial.begin(9600);
}


void loop() {
  readingA0 = analogRead(PinA0);
  Serial.print("Raw input: ");
  // If you want to use serial plotter comment out the Serial.print(readingA0)line
  Serial.print(readingA0);
  float voltage = readingA0 * (5.0 / 1023.0); //use Arduino for input of voltage, do not use
              // external voltage.  Unless you are very sure of what you are doing.
  Serial.print(" Voltage: ");
  Serial.println(voltage,3); //display with 3 decimal places
  delay(2000);          //approx 2 seconds
}
```

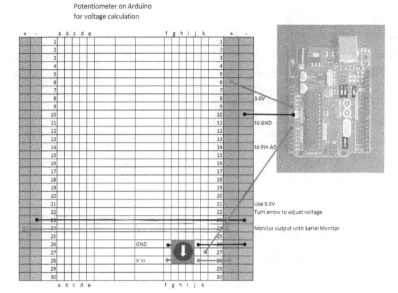

Potentiometer on Arduino
for voltage calculation

5.0V
to GND
to Pin A0

Use 5.0V
Turn arrow to adjust voltage

Monitor output with Serial Monitor

GND
V in

C:\Users\Herb\Documents\BOOKSpublish\Arduino Projects\[ArduinoProjects.xlsx]PotentiometerVoltage

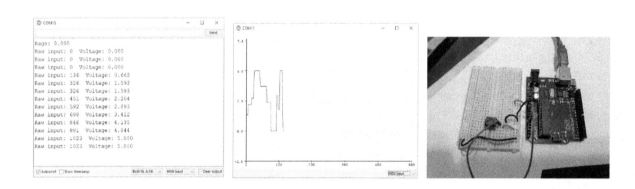

Project 4: Tactile Button/Switch

This program counts the number of times you press the Tactile Button. The count is displayed on the IDE Serial Monitor. We used two 220Ω resistors, the exact value is not required. One resistor takes the bounce out of the button. Second resistor to protect LED.

```
/* Arduino_Tactile_Button   Herb Norbom 4/4/2019  LED on/off when button pressed,
   display on serial monitor number of times button pressed.
   LED attached to pin 8 and ground with resistor
   pushbutton attached to pin 3 from +3.3V
   220 ohm resistor attached to Button pin 2 and ground
*/
int buttonPin = 3;    // number of the pushbutton pin
int ledPin =  8;      // number of the LED pin
int button3State = 0;       // variable for reading the pushbutton status
int buttonPressedCounter =0; //counter number of times button pressed
void setup() {
  Serial.begin(9600);
```

```
  Serial.println("Ready to count");
  pinMode(ledPin, OUTPUT); //set LED pin output
  pinMode(buttonPin, INPUT);//set button as input
}

void loop() {
  button3State = digitalRead(buttonPin); //read state
  if (button3State == HIGH) { //pressed is HIGH state turn LED on
    digitalWrite(ledPin, HIGH);
    buttonPressedCounter +=1;
    Serial.println(buttonPressedCounter);
    delay(200);                 // waits 200ms to take bounce out of button
  }
  else {
    digitalWrite(ledPin, LOW); //not pressed turn LED off
  }
}
```

Tactile Button/Switch
for on/off LED

The program counts number of times button pressed.
LED on when button pressed.

Use resistor or LED may burn out

3.3V

to GND

to Pin 8

to Pin 3

GND

V in

Run at 3.3V to minimize possible damage.

Need resistor to take bounce out of button
In this example using 2   220Ω 10% resistors
                    red,red,brown,silver

COM12 (Arduino/Genuino Uno)

Ready to count
1
2
3
4

Project 5: Temperature/Humidity

This program uses a combination sensor for measuring Temperature and Humidity (DHT11). The results are displayed on the IDE Serial Monitor. We have also included a Photo Light Sensor for displaying light on/off information.

The DHT11 requires the Adafruit library. https://www.adafruit.com/product/386 and https://learn.adafruit.com/dht/downloads. The actual library is at https://github.com/adafruit/Adafruit_Sensor. The library is free. Download the "DHT-sensor-library-master.zip". To install:

- Under the IDE select "Sketch"
- Include library
- Add Zip library
- select the downloaded file "DHT-sensor-master-zip"
- Once installed "DHT Sensor Library" will show under "Sketch/Include library/Recommended Libraries" as "DHT Sensor Library"

The "Adafruit_Sensor" library is not required for this project, but it is a good library to have installed. Follow same procedure as before and link to https://github.com/adafruit/Adafruit_Sensor

```
/* Arduino_Temp_Humidity   Herb Norbom 4/2/2018
  DHT Temperature & Humidity Sensor with Photo sensor
  REQUIRES the following Arduino libraries:// - DHT Sensor Library: https://github.com/adafruit/DHT-sensor-library
  Adafruit Unified Sensor Lib: https://github.com/adafruit/Adafruit_Sensor (Not required for this project)
*/
//#include <Adafruit_Sensor.h>
#include <DHT.h>
#include <DHT_U.h>
#define DHTPIN 2         // Digital pin connected to the DHT sensor
#define DHTTYPE   DHT11
DHT_Unified dht(DHTPIN, DHTTYPE);
int light_on_off = 0;   // on = 1, off = 0
//PhotoCell
const int photocellPin = 0;    // the cell and 10K pulldown are connected to a0
int photocellReading;    // the analog reading from the sensor divider

void setup() {
  Serial.begin(9600);
  dht.begin();
  sensor_t sensor;
  dht.temperature().getSensor(&sensor);
}
void loop() {
  delay(5000);
  photocellReading = analogRead(photocellPin); // Get Photo Cell Reading
// Serial.println(photocellReading);  // analog reading for setting threshold
  if (photocellReading <= 600)  {light_on_off = 0;} //light off, below threshold
  else {   light_on_off = 1;}     //light on
  sensors_event_t event;   // Get temperature event and print its value.
  dht.temperature().getEvent(&event);
```

```
Serial.print("Centigrate: ");
Serial.print(event.temperature);  // centigrate
Serial.print(" Fahrenheit: ");
Serial.print((event.temperature * 1.8) + 32);  //fahrenheit
Serial.print(" Humidity: ");
dht.humidity().getEvent(&event);    // Get humidity event and print its value.
Serial.print(event.relative_humidity);
Serial.print(" Light:  ");
if (light_on_off == 1){Serial.println("ON");}
if (light_on_off == 0){Serial.println("OFF");}}
```

Temperature/Humidity Sensor DHT11
Photocell for light on/off detection

10kΩ10%
Brown,Black,Orange,Silver
(came with temp sensor)

Adafruit DHT11 part 386

VCC
signal
not used
GND

Photocell (CdS photoresistor)
Adafruit PID: 161 $0.95
to 5V rail
to resistor and Pin A0

C:\Users\Herb\Documents\BOOKSpublish\Arduino Projects\[ArduinoProjects.xlsx]Temp_Humidity

Project 6: Temperature/Humidity with Fan

This project adds a fan to the previous project. The low voltage/amperage fan is controlled by an H-Bridge. Just using ¼ of the H-Bridge for this project. You need a small resistor from Pin 9 of the H-Bridge to Ground. Without this resistor the fan may not turn off. From the Arduino we will be using PWM pin 11 to enable the H-Bridge. The PWM pulse controls the speed of the fan. Fan speed is adjusted based on the temperature. The program contains a testing feature for the PWM fan where you should see the speed adjust. The photo light sensor used in the previous project has been removed

```
/*  Arduino_Temp_Humidity_with_FANPWM   Herb Norbom 4/2/2019
    REQUIRES the following Arduino libraries:// - DHT Sensor Library: https://github.com/adafruit/DHT-sensor-library
*/
#include <DHT.h>
#include <DHT_U.h>
#define DHTPIN 2          // Digital pin connected to the DHT sensor
#define DHTTYPE    DHT11
DHT_Unified dht(DHTPIN, DHTTYPE);

#define enableMotorR 11     // Enable H-Bridge pin 11, this is pwm pin speed 0 to 255
#define RightRev  7
#define RightFwd  6

int speed = 0;
float Ftemp=0.0;
char inChar =0;
int x =0;

void setup() {
  Serial.begin(9600);
  Serial.println("Starting");
  pinMode(enableMotorR, OUTPUT);
  pinMode(RightRev, OUTPUT);
  pinMode(RightFwd, OUTPUT);
  digitalWrite(RightRev, LOW);
  digitalWrite(RightFwd, LOW);
  dht.begin();
  sensor_t sensor;
  dht.temperature().getSensor(&sensor);
  }

void loop() {
  if ( Serial.available()>0){
   inChar = Serial.read();
   Serial.println(inChar);
    if(inChar=='g'){
      Serial.println("turn ON");
      digitalWrite(RightRev, HIGH);
      digitalWrite(RightFwd, LOW);
      for (x = 75; x <250;x = x + 5){
        Serial.println(x);
        analogWrite(enableMotorR, x);
        delay(200);
```

```arduino
    }
    for (x = 255; x >75;x = x -5){
      Serial.println(x);
      analogWrite(enableMotorR, x);
      delay(200);
    }
  }
}
inChar="";
sensors_event_t event;    // Get temperature event
dht.temperature().getEvent(&event);
Ftemp=  (event.temperature * 1.8) + 32;
Serial.print(" Fahrenheit: ");
Serial.print(Ftemp);
Serial.print(" Humidity: ");
dht.humidity().getEvent(&event);    // Get humidity event
Serial.println(event.relative_humidity);
if (Ftemp > 74.0){
  Serial.print("FAN speed: ");
  speed = map(Ftemp,74.0,94.0,125,255);//use f in range 71.0 to 94.0 map
                // pwm 125 to 255
                // pwm min needs to be > than motor stall speed
  Serial.println(speed);
  analogWrite(enableMotorR, speed);
  digitalWrite(RightRev, HIGH);
  digitalWrite(RightFwd, LOW);
}
if (Ftemp <= 74.0){
  Serial.println("FAN OFF");
  digitalWrite(RightRev, LOW);
  digitalWrite(RightFwd, LOW);
}
delay(1000);
}
```

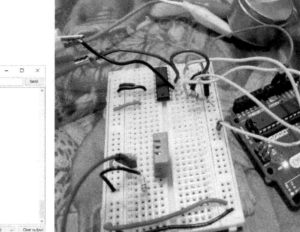

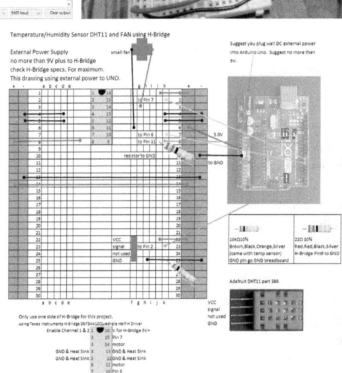

Temperature/Humidity Sensor DHT11 and FAN using H-Bridge

External Power Supply
no more than 9V plus to H-Bridge
check H-Bridge specs. For maximum.
This drawing using external power to UNO.

small fan

Suggest you plug wall DC external power
into Arduino Uno. Suggest no more than
9V.

to Pin 7

to Pin 6
to Pin 11

resistor to GND

5.0V

to GND

VCC
signal   to Pin 2
not used
GND

10kΩ10%
Brown,Black,Orange,Silver
(came with temp sensor)
GND pin go GND breadboard

22Ω 10%
Red,Red,Black,Silver
H-Bridge Pin9 to GND

VCC
signal
not used
GND

Adafruit DHT11 part 386

Only use one side of H-Bridge for this project.
using Texas Instruments H-Bridge SN754410Quadruple Half-H Driver

Enable Channel 1 & 2	1	16	V for H-Bridge 5V+	
	2	15	Pin 7	
	3	14	motor	
GND & Heat Sink	4	13	GND & Heat Sink	
GND & Heat Sink	5	12	GND & Heat Sink	
	6	11	motor	
	7	10	Pin 6	
V + for Motor	8	9	Enable Channel 3 & 4 Pin 11 on Arduino	

Project 7 Soil Moisture Sensor with pump

Building on what we have learned. Use a Soil Moisture Sensor to control a pump. In this program the lower the reading the more moisture detected. The pump is set to turn on when the moisture level reading is greater than 951. This project could be used to control a small plant watering system.

```
/*  Arduino_MoistureSensor_Pump_PWM   Herb Norbom 4/4/2019
    reguires Soil Moisture Sensor Kit, H-Bridge and Small Pump
*/
int sensorA0=0;        // variable to store moisture sensor reading
```

```
#define enableMotorR 11     // Enable H-Bridge pin 11,this is pwm pin speed 0 to 255
#define RightRev  7
#define RightFwd  6
int speed = 0;
char inChar =0;
int x =0;

void setup() {
 Serial.begin(9600);
 Serial.println("Starting");
 pinMode(enableMotorR, OUTPUT);
 pinMode(RightRev, OUTPUT);
 pinMode(RightFwd, OUTPUT);
 digitalWrite(RightRev, LOW);
 digitalWrite(RightFwd, LOW);
 }

void loop() {
 if ( Serial.available()>0){
  inChar = Serial.read();
  Serial.println(inChar);
   if(inChar=='g'){             // for testing pump
    Serial.println("turn ON");
    digitalWrite(RightRev, HIGH);
    digitalWrite(RightFwd, LOW);
    for (x = 75; x <250;x = x + 5){
     Serial.println(x);
     analogWrite(enableMotorR, x);
     delay(200);
    }
    for (x = 255; x >75;x = x -5){
     Serial.println(x);
     analogWrite(enableMotorR, x);
     delay(200);
    }
  }
 }
 inChar="";
 getReading();
 if (sensorA0 >= 951){
   Serial.print("PUMP ON speed: ");
   speed = map(sensorA0,950,450,125,255);//use sensorA0 in range 950 to 450 for map
         // pwm 125 to 255, pwm min needs to be > than motor stall speed
   Serial.println(speed);
   analogWrite(enableMotorR, speed);
```

```
    digitalWrite(RightRev, HIGH);
    digitalWrite(RightFwd, LOW);
  }

  if (sensorA0 < 950){
    Serial.println("PUMP OFF");
    digitalWrite(RightRev, LOW);
    digitalWrite(RightFwd, LOW);
  }
  delay(1000);
}


void getReading(){
  sensorA0 = analogRead(0);
  Serial.println(sensorA0);
}
```

Soil Moisture Sensor with Pump

External Power Supply
no more than 9V plus to H-Bridge
check H-Bridge specs. For maximum.
This drawing using external power to UNO.

small pump

Suggest you plug wall DC external power
into Arduino Uno. Suggest no more than
9V.

to Pin 7

to Pin 6
to Pin 11

resistor to GND

5.0V

to GND

Signal to Pin A0

22Ω 10%
Red,Red,Black,Silver
H-Bridge Pin9 to GND

VCC
GND
not used
Signal to A0

Only use one side of H-Bridge for this project.
using Texas Instruments H-Bridge SN754410Quadrple Half-H Driver

Enable Channel 1 & 2	1	16	V for H-Bridge 5V+
	2	15	Pin 7
	3	14	motor
GND & Heat Sink	4	13	GND & Heat Sink
GND & Heat Sink	5	12	GND & Heat Sink
	6	11	motor
	7	10	Pin 6
V + for Motor	8	9	Enable Channel 3 & 4 Pin 11 on Arduino

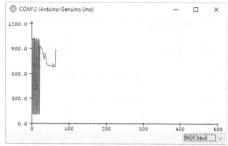

You can also use the Serial Plotter to track readings.

Project 8 LCD Display

We will be using a 16x4 LCD display that uses the Hitachi HD44780 Driver. This code and wiring should work with any 16 pin LCD using the Hitachi driver. With minor changes to the code you can use a 16x2 and other sizes supported by the Liquid Crystal Library. (We are not going into the i2c type of Liquid Crystal until a later project.)

The Liquid Crystal library greatly simplifies coding. See https://www.arduino.cc/en/Reference/LiquidCrystal and https://arduinoliquidcrystal.readthedocs.io/en/latest/liquidcrystal.html for a description of features.

This project demonstrates some of the Liquid Crystal Library commands. We have also included a serial input so that you can enter some information on the fly. This LCD can accept up to 20 characters per line. You may want to change the code to accommodate your LCD.

```
/* Arduino_LCD_Display  Herb Norbom 4/4/2019
 Using a 16x4 LCD display.  The LiquidCrystal
 library works with all LCD displays that are compatible with the
 Hitachi HD44780 driver. There are many of them out there, and you
 can usually tell them by the 16-pin interface.
 */

#include <LiquidCrystal.h>
/*
16 pin LCD
LCD pin
 1 GND
 2 5V
 3 middle pin potentiometer
```

```
    4 rs  Arduino pin 7
    5 rw GND  (not writting from LCD)
    6 en  Arduino pin 8
    7 n/a
    8 n/a
    9 n/a
    10 n/a
    11 DB4  Arduino pin 9
    12 DB5  Arduino pin 10
    13 DB6  Arduino pin 11
    14 DB7  Arduino pin 12
    15 Arduino pin 5V
    16 Arduino pin GND
    */
//          rs,en,d4,d5, d6, d7
LiquidCrystal lcd(7, 8, 9, 10, 11, 12); //Arduino Digital Pins
// depending on your LCD you may need to change pins
int inputCounter = 0;
char inChar ="";
String inputString="";
boolean stringComplete = false;

void setup() {
  Serial.begin(9600);
  lcd.begin(20, 4);   // change as needed, typical is two lines 16 characters (16,2)
              //  This LCD has four lines and 20 characters
  lcd.print("Arduino LCD project"); //note this displays on row 0 column 1
  lcd.setCursor(5,2);  // column 5 row 3, note LCDstarts with row 0
  lcd.print("Hi Herb");
  lcd.setCursor(9,3);  // column 9 row 4, note LCDstarts with row 0
  lcd.print("Good Job");
  for (int counter =0; counter<10; counter++){
   lcd.scrollDisplayLeft();
   delay(225);
  }
  for (int counter =0; counter<10; counter++){
   lcd.scrollDisplayRight();
   delay(225);
  }
}

void loop() {
 if (stringComplete){
   lcd.clear();
   inputString.trim();
```

```
    inputCounter = inputString.length();
    Serial.println(inputCounter);
    if (inputCounter > 20){
      inputCounter = 20;
    }
    for( int counter=0; counter<inputCounter; counter++){
      lcd.setCursor(counter,1);
      lcd.print(inputString[counter]);
    }
      Serial.println(inputString);
   stringComplete = false;
   inputString="";
  }
}
void serialEvent() {
 while (Serial.available()) {
  char inChar = (char)Serial.read();
  inputString += inChar;
  if (inChar == '\n') {
    stringComplete = true;
  }
 }
}
```

Arduino LCD Display
using 16 pin with Hitachi HD44780 Driver

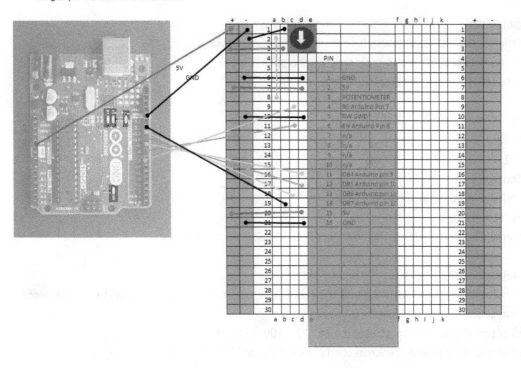

Notice how input cut from Serial when displayed on the LCD.

Project 9 Ultra-sonic Sensor

Using the Ultra-Sonic Sensor (HC-SR04) for measuring distance in Centimeters and Inches. A warning light flashes if under 4.0 inches. We are using 5V to power the Ultra-Sonic Sensor. Use the appropriate resistor for the LED. Distances are displayed on the IDE Serial Monitor. Try the plotter also.

```
//Arduino_Ultra_Sonic    Herb Norbom 4/5/2019 also use plotter
#define echoPin  8 // Echo Pin
#define trigPin  7 // Trigger Pin
#define LED 2      //LED Flash
long Duration;
float Distance_cm, Distance_in; // use float want decimals for distance
//char inChar =0;   //set monitor as default
//int Display = 0;   //set monitor=0 as default, 1=Plotter
int Display = 1;   //set monitor=0 as default, 1=Plotter
void setup(){
  Serial.begin(9600);       // serial communication 9600 baud.
  pinMode(trigPin, OUTPUT); //ultrasonic sensor trigger pin as output.
  pinMode(echoPin, INPUT);   //ultrasonic sensor echo pin as input.
  pinMode(LED, OUTPUT);     // LED pin for Flash
}
void loop(){
  UltraSensed();
  delay(750);}
void UltraSensed(){
  digitalWrite(trigPin, LOW); // Clears the trigPin
  delayMicroseconds(2);
  digitalWrite(trigPin, HIGH); // Sets trigPin to HIGH for 10 micro seconds
  delayMicroseconds(10);
  digitalWrite(trigPin, LOW);
  Duration = pulseIn(echoPin, HIGH); // Reads the echoPin, returns the sound wave travel time microseconds
     // speed of sound in meters/Second = 343.21
     // speed of sound in centimeters/Second = 343.21 * 100 = 34,321
     // speed of sound centimeters/Microsecond = 34,321 / 1,000,000 = 0.034321
     //convert to centimeters to inches 34,321 * 0.393701 =  13,512.2120
     // speed of sound inches/Microsecond = 13,512.2120 / 1,000,000 = 0.01351221
```

```
Distance_in = Duration * 0.01351221/2; //Distance in inches speed of sound/Microsecond.
if (Display==1){
  if (Distance_in >10.0){
    Distance_in =10.0;
  }
  Serial.println(Distance_in, 1);
}
if (Display==0){
  Serial.print("Distance ");  Serial.print("INCHES "); Serial.print(Distance_in, 1); // 1 decimal position
  Distance_cm = Duration*0.034321/2; //Distance in centimeters/Microsecond
  Serial.print(" Centimeters: "); Serial.println(Distance_cm, 2); // 2 decimal positions
}
if (Distance_in <4.0){
  Flash();
}
}

void Flash(){
  digitalWrite(LED, HIGH);
  Serial.println("**WARNING**");
  delay(1000);
  digitalWrite(LED, LOW);
}
```

Arduino
using UltraSonic Sensor HC-SR04

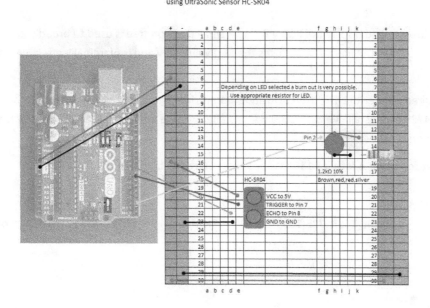

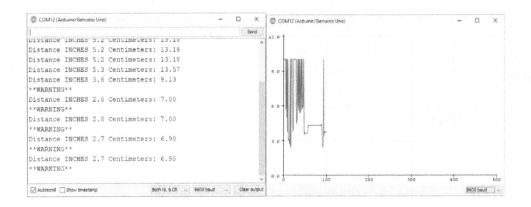

Project 10 Color Identifier

With this project we identify and display the RGB values. A small decision tree is used to broadly identify (RED, GREEN, BLACK, and YELLOW). The identification uses the RED value only and is marginally effective. We are sure you can refine.

Free software is required. Under the IDE 'Sketch/Include Library/Manage Libraries' enter "tcs" in the search field. Select Adafruit TCS34725 and install. Version 1.3.0 was installed. There are several sample programs included. The following is based on one of those sketches.

```
// Arduino_Color_Sensor  using Adafruit P1334 Color Sensor Herb Norbom 4/5/2019
#include <Wire.h>
#include "Adafruit_TCS34725.h"
Adafruit_TCS34725 tcs = Adafruit_TCS34725(TCS34725_INTEGRATIONTIME_50MS, TCS34725_GAIN_4X);

void setup() {
 Serial.begin(9600);
 if (tcs.begin()) {
 } else {
  Serial.println("No TCS34725 found ... check your connections");
  while (1); // halt!
 }
}
```

```
void loop() {
 float red, green, blue;
 tcs.setInterrupt(false);  // turn on LED
 delay(60);  // takes 50ms to read
 tcs.getRGB(&red, &green, &blue);
 Serial.print("R:\t"); Serial.print(int(red));
 Serial.print("\tG:\t"); Serial.print(int(green));
 Serial.print("\tB:\t"); Serial.print(int(blue));
 Serial.print("\n");
 if ((red>=176) and (red <= 181)){
  Serial.println("Color is RED");}
 if ((red>=33) and (red <= 74)){
  Serial.println("Color is GREEN");}
 if ((red>=94) and (red <= 112)){
  Serial.println("Color is BLACK");}
 if ((red>=122) and (red <= 133)){
  Serial.println("Color is YELLOW");}
}
```

Arduino
using TCS34725 Color Sensor from Adafruit P1334

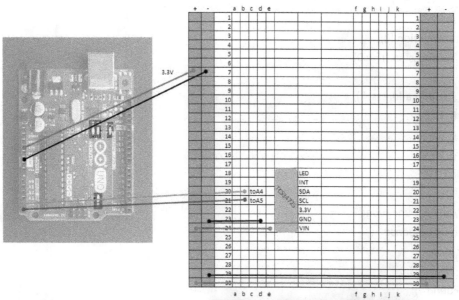

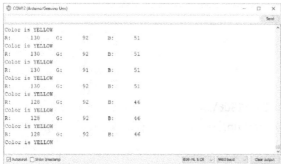

Using a small OLED "Organic Light Emitting Diode" 128x64 (approx. 1.3" x 1.3") I2C interface. There are several available on eBay and check out Adafruit also. Many of them have different pin outs. We are running using 3.3V, many will accept 5V.

You do need to install two FREE libraries made available by Adafruit.

https://github.com/adafruit/Adafruit_SSD1306 and https://github.com/adafruit/Adafruit-GFX-Library

Once the libraries are installed select the example ('File/Examples/Adafruit SSD1306_128x64_i2c'). Compile and run. As you will note in the wiring diagram, we did not connect a reset pin.

To get the I2C address we ran the following small program.

```
// I2C Scanner From Internet author unknown
#include <Wire.h>
void setup() {
 Serial.begin (9600);
 Serial.println ();
 Serial.println ("I2C scanner. Scanning ...");
 byte count = 0;
 Wire.begin();
 for (byte i = 1; i < 120; i++)
 {
  Wire.beginTransmission (i);
  if (Wire.endTransmission () == 0)
   {
   Serial.print ("Found address: ");
   Serial.print (i, DEC);
   Serial.print (" (0x");
   Serial.print (i, HEX);
   Serial.println (")");
   count++;
   delay (1);  // maybe unneeded?
   } // end of good response
 } // end of for loop
 Serial.println ("Done.");
 Serial.print ("Found ");
 Serial.print (count, DEC);
 Serial.println (" device(s).");
} // end of setup
void loop() {}
```

With the correct address in the script run 'File\Examples\Adafruit\SSD\1306\ssd1306_128x64_i2c'. This demo program produces a wide range of displays. This took a minute to start up. The screen was dark until it got going.

Arduino
1.3" 128x64 OLED I2C Serial LED LCD Screen. Display Module for Arduino Blue.

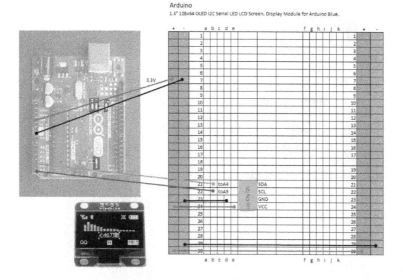

https://www.ebay.com/itm/1-3-128X64-OLED-I2C-IIC-Serial-LED-LCD-Screen-Display-Module-for-Arduino-Blue/282415392907?epid=7002879598&hash=item41c144ec8a:g:G-AAQSwScNYNLGM

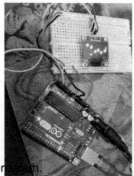

You may need to change the address in the test program.

Program to accept Serial Monitor input and display on the OLED.

//Arduino_OLED_Hello   With Serial Monitor input displayed on OLED
/***

This is an example for our Monochrome OLEDs based on SSD1306 drivers

Pick one up today in the adafruit shop!

------> http://www.adafruit.com/category/63_98

Adafruit invests time and resources providing this open

source code, please support Adafruit and open-source

hardware by purchasing products from Adafruit!

Written by Limor Fried/Ladyada for Adafruit Industries,

with contributions from the open source community.

BSD license, check license.txt for more information

All text above, and the splash screen below must be

included in any redistribution.

****

Modifed Herb Norbom for Serial Monitor input/display 11/22/2019

```
*/
#include <Wire.h>
#include <Adafruit_GFX.h>
#include <Adafruit_SSD1306.h>
#define SCREEN_WIDTH 128 // OLED display width, in pixels
#define SCREEN_HEIGHT 64 // OLED display height, in pixels
// Declaration for an SSD1306 display connected to I2C (SDA, SCL pins)
#define OLED_RESET    4 // Reset pin # (or -1 if sharing Arduino reset pin)
Adafruit_SSD1306 display(SCREEN_WIDTH, SCREEN_HEIGHT, &Wire, OLED_RESET);

String inputString="";
boolean stringComplete = false;

void setup() {
  Serial.begin(9600);
  Serial.println("Starting..Enter your message");
  inputString.reserve(200);
  // SSD1306_SWITCHCAPVCC = generate display voltage from 3.3V internally
  if(!display.begin(SSD1306_SWITCHCAPVCC, 0x3C)) { // Address 0x3C for 128x64
    Serial.println(F("SSD1306 allocation failed"));
    for(;;); // Don't proceed, loop forever
  }
  // Show initial display buffer contents on the screen --
  // the library initializes this with an Adafruit splash screen.
//  display.display();   //uncomment to see Adafruit Name on OLED
  delay(2000); // Pause for 2 seconds
}

void loop() {
  display.clearDisplay();
  display.setTextColor(WHITE);  //required even though display is blue
  display.setTextSize(1);
  display.setCursor(0,0);
  display.print("Hello Good Looking!");
  display.setCursor(0,10);
  display.print("very interesting");
  display.display();
  if (stringComplete){
```

```
      display.setCursor(0,20);
      display.print(inputString);
      inputString="";
      display.display();
      delay(5000);   //time to read before cleared
   }
}
void serialEvent() {
  while (Serial.available()) {
    char inChar = (char)Serial.read();     // get the new byte
    inputString += inChar;            // add it to the inputString
    // if the incoming character is a newline, set a flag
    // so the main loop can write to file
    if (inChar == '\n') {
      stringComplete = true;
    }
  }
}
```

Project 12 SD Card

When you need more storage look to a SD Card. A lot easier to use than you might expect. We are not sure where we purchased our Micro SD Card Adapter Reader SPI interface. We are using an 8Gb Micro Card, FAT 16.

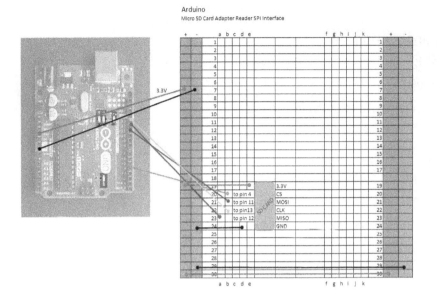

Arduino
Micro SD Card Adapter Reader SPI Interface

After you have inserted a SD card and wired the adapter try to run the sample program included with the IDE. From the IDE 'File\Examples\SD\Card Info'.

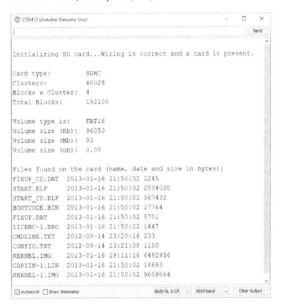

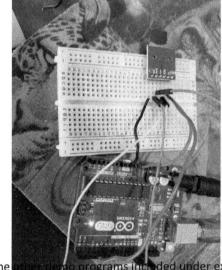

With the Arduino recognizing the SD card try some of the other demo programs included under examples. From the IDE 'File\Examples\SD\ReadWrite' and 'File\Examples\SD\listfiles'. The output is shown in the following. Notice our new 'TEST.TXT' file.

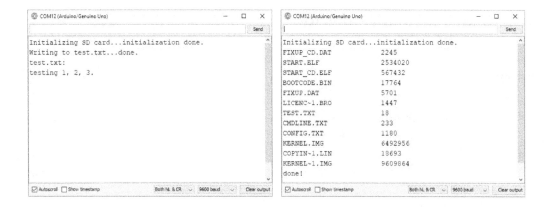

More information on the SD options available at https://www.arduino.cc/en/Reference/SD.

Several programs follow based on above to show input of a file name and writing to that file. Reading a file, input the file name. Deleting a file.

Project 13 SD Write to file

```
/* Arduino_SD_Write_Serial_Input  Herb Norbom 4/7/2019
 based on example  by David A. Mellis modified 9 Apr 2012 and Tom Igoe
 */
#include <SPI.h>
#include <SD.h>
File myFile;
String fileName;
String inputString="";
boolean stringComplete = false;
boolean fileNameEntered = false;

void setup() {
  Serial.begin(9600);
  Serial.println("Starting");
  inputString.reserve(200);
  Serial.print("Initializing SD card...");
  if (!SD.begin(4)) {
    Serial.println("initialization failed!");
    while (1);
  }
  Serial.println("initialization done.");
  Serial.println("Enter File Name: ");
}

void loop() {
  if (fileNameEntered == false){
    if (stringComplete){
      fileName= inputString;
      int len = fileName.length();
```

```
      fileName.remove(len-2,2);// Serial monitor adds 'Both NL & CR' adjust if different setting
      inputString="";
      stringComplete = false;
      Serial.println(fileName);
      fileNameEntered = true;
      myFile = SD.open(fileName.c_str(), FILE_WRITE);
      if (myFile) {
        Serial.println("file opened");
      } else {
        Serial.print("error opening: ");
        Serial.println(myFile);
      }
    }
  }
  if (stringComplete){
    fileName= inputString;
    Serial.println(inputString);
    stringComplete = false;
    if (myFile) {
      int tempChar = myFile.println(inputString); //returns number of chars written
      Serial.print("Chars written: ");
      Serial.println(tempChar);
      inputString="";
      myFile.close();
      Serial.println("File Closed");
    } else {
      Serial.print("error opening: ");
      Serial.println(fileName);
    }
  }
}
void serialEvent() {
  while (Serial.available()) {
    char inChar = (char)Serial.read();    // get the new byte
    inputString += inChar;               // add it to the inputString
    // if the incoming character is a newline, set a flag
    // so the main loop can write to file
    if (inChar == '\n') {
      stringComplete = true;
    }
  }
}
```

You may notice that some line feeds and carriage returns are included in the number of characters written.

Project 14 SD List Dir and Read File

/*Arduino_SD_List_Files_Read Herb Norbom 4/7/2019

created   Nov 2010 by David A. Mellis, modified 9 Apr 2012 by Tom Igoe

modified 2 Feb 2014 by Scott Fitzgerald

 modified 4/7/2019 Herb Norbom

This example code is in the public domain.

*/

```
#include <SPI.h>
#include <SD.h>

File root;
File myFile;
String fileName;
String inputString="";
boolean stringComplete = false;
void setup() {
 // Open serial communications and wait for port to open:
 Serial.begin(9600);
 while (!Serial) {
  ; // wait for serial port to connect. Needed for native USB port only
 }
 Serial.print("Initializing SD card...");
 if (!SD.begin(4)) {
  Serial.println("initialization failed!");
  while (1);
 }
 Serial.println("initialization done.");
 root = SD.open("/");
 printDirectory(root, 0);
 Serial.println("done!");
 Serial.println("Enter File Name: ");
}
```

```
void loop() {
 if (stringComplete){
  stringComplete = false;
  fileName= inputString;
  int len = fileName.length();
  fileName.remove(len-2,2);// Serial monitor adds 'Both NL & CR' adjust if different setting
  Serial.println("Opening file");
  myFile = SD.open(fileName.c_str());   // re-open the file for reading
  Serial.println();
  if (myFile) {
   while (myFile.available()) {
   Serial.write(myFile.read());
   }
   myFile.close();
  } else {
   Serial.print("error opening: ");
   Serial.println(fileName);
  }
 }
}

void printDirectory(File dir, int numTabs) {
 while (true) {
  File entry =  dir.openNextFile();
  if (! entry) {
   // no more files
   break;
  }
  for (uint8_t i = 0; i < numTabs; i++) {
   Serial.print('\t');
  }
  Serial.print(entry.name());
  if (entry.isDirectory()) {
   Serial.println("/");
   printDirectory(entry, numTabs + 1);
  } else {
   // files have sizes, directories do not
   Serial.print("\t\t");
   Serial.println(entry.size(), DEC);
  }
  entry.close();
 }
}
void serialEvent() {
 while (Serial.available()) {
```

```
  char inChar = (char)Serial.read();     // get the new byte
  inputString += inChar;                 // add it to the inputString
  // if the incoming character is a newline, set a flag
  // so the main loop can write to file
  if (inChar == '\n') {
    stringComplete = true;
  }
 }
}
```

Project 15 SD Remove File

```
/*Arduino_SD_RemoveFile  Herb Norbom 4/7/2019
 created   Nov 2010 by David A. Mellis, modified 9 Apr 2012 by Tom Igoe
 modified 2 Feb 2014 by Scott Fitzgerald
  modified 4/7/2019 Herb Norbom
 This example code is in the public domain.
 */
#include <SPI.h>
#include <SD.h>

File root;
File myFile;
String fileName;
String inputString="";
boolean stringComplete = false;
void setup() {
 Serial.begin(9600);
 Serial.print("Initializing SD card...");
 if (!SD.begin(4)) {
  Serial.println("initialization failed!");
   while (1);
 }
 Serial.println("initialization done.");
 root = SD.open("/");
 printDirectory(root, 0);
```

```
  Serial.println("Directory done!");
  Serial.println("Enter File Name: ");
}

void loop() {
 if (stringComplete){
  stringComplete = false;
  fileName= inputString;
  int len = fileName.length();
  fileName.remove(len-2,2);// Serial monitor adds 'Both NL & CR' adjust if different setting
  Serial.print("Removing file: ");
  Serial.println(fileName);
  SD.remove(fileName.c_str());   // delete file from SD

  if (SD.exists(fileName.c_str())){
   Serial.println("Error file not removed");
  } else{
   Serial.println("File not found or removed");
  }
 }
}

void printDirectory(File dir, int numTabs) {
 while (true) {

  File entry =  dir.openNextFile();
  if (! entry) {
   // no more files
   break;
  }
  for (uint8_t i = 0; i < numTabs; i++) {
   Serial.print('\t');
  }
  Serial.print(entry.name());
  if (entry.isDirectory()) {
   Serial.println("/");
   printDirectory(entry, numTabs + 1);
  } else {
   // files have sizes, directories do not
   Serial.print("\t\t");
   Serial.println(entry.size(), DEC);
  }
  entry.close();
 }
}
```

```
void serialEvent() {
  while (Serial.available()) {
    char inChar = (char)Serial.read();     // get the new byte
    inputString += inChar;               // add it to the inputString
    // if the incoming character is a newline, set a flag
    // so the main loop can write to file
    if (inChar == '\n') {
      stringComplete = true;
    }
  }
}
```

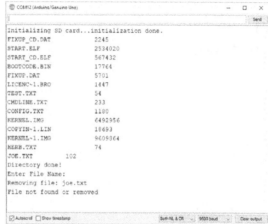

Project 16 SD Card File List and Play Wav File

Wanting our robots to play sound bites was the main reason we looked at the SD card. In this example we had some inexpensive speakers that have a battery amplifier built in. You will need an amplifier. There are various amplifiers available on Amazon, eBay and instructions on the web. The free software TMRpcm is required. Easiest method to install it is with Arduino Library Manager (Sketch\Include Library\Manage Libraries). Enter "tmrpcm" in the search field, select and install.

We did not run with any "pcm" files, "wav "files work well. Once installed there are examples. You will need to copy "wav" files to the SD. The following script provides a directory of the SD. You enter the file name and the file plays.

```
// Arduino_SD_WAV_LIST_FILES  Herb Norbom 4/8/2019
#include <SD.h>          // need to include the SD library
#include <TMRpcm.h>        //  also need to include this library...
File root;
File myFile;
```

```
String fileName;
String inputString="";
boolean stringComplete = false;
TMRpcm tmrpcm;   // create an object for use in this sketch

void setup(){
 tmrpcm.speakerPin = 9; //output to speaker
 Serial.begin(9600);
 if (!SD.begin(4)) {  // Initializing SD card
  Serial.println("SD fail");
  return;  // don't do anything more if not found
 }
 Serial.println("initialization done.");
 root = SD.open("/");     // need to get directory of SD
 printDirectory(root, 0);
 Serial.println("done!");
 Serial.println("Enter File Name: ");
}

void loop(){
 if (stringComplete){
  stringComplete = false;
  fileName= inputString;
  int len = fileName.length();
  fileName.remove(len-2,2);// Serial monitor adds 'Both NL & CR' adjust if different setting
  Serial.println("Opening file");
  myFile = SD.open(fileName.c_str());  // re-open the file for reading
  Serial.println();
  if (myFile) {
   tmrpcm.play(fileName.c_str());
  }
 }
}

void printDirectory(File dir, int numTabs) {
 while (true) {
  File entry = dir.openNextFile();
  if (! entry) {
   // no more files
   break;
  }
  for (uint8_t i = 0; i < numTabs; i++) {
   Serial.print('\t');
  }
  Serial.print(entry.name());
```

```
  if (entry.isDirectory()) {
    Serial.println("/");
    printDirectory(entry, numTabs + 1);
  } else {
    // files have sizes, directories do not
    Serial.print("\t\t");
    Serial.println(entry.size(), DEC);
  }
  entry.close();
 }
}
void serialEvent() {
 while (Serial.available()) {
  char inChar = (char)Serial.read();     // get the new byte
  inputString += inChar;            // add it to the inputString
  // if the incoming character is a newline, set a flag
  // so the main loop can write to file
  if (inChar == '\n') {
    stringComplete = true;
   }
  }
}
```

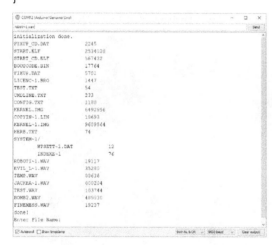

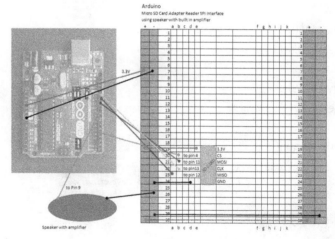

Project 17 Thumb Joystick

A quick project to use a small Joystick. The analog pins are used to read the voltage from x and y axis. We set some arbitrary values for direction based on our reading. We are sure you can refine. The SW or button press was found to be too erratic to use, at least with our Thumb Joystick.

```
/* Arduino_Thumb_Joystick  Herb Norbom 4/8/2019
 * Analog pins on UNO receive X, Y positions
 * A0 X axis, full left = 0, Center =513, full right = 1023
 * A1 Y axis, full up = 0, Center =485, full down = 1023
 */
```

```
int x = 0;          // value from the analog pin 0
int y = 0;          // value from the analog pin 1

void setup() {
 Serial.begin(9600);
 Serial.println("Starting...");
 }

void loop() {
 delay(300);
 x = analogRead(0);       // analog pin 0
 delay(100);
 y = analogRead(1);       // analog pin 1
 Serial.print("  X axis ");
 Serial.print(x);
 Serial.print("  Y axis ");
 Serial.print(y);
 if (x <=500){
  Serial.print("  Left");
 }
 if (x >=520){
  Serial.print("  Right");
 }
 if (y <=450){
  Serial.print("  Forward");
 }
 if (y >=505){
  Serial.print("  Reverse");
 }
 Serial.println("");
 }
```

Arduino with Thumb Joystick
https://www.adafruit.com/product/512

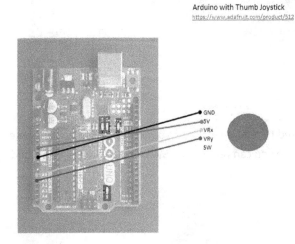

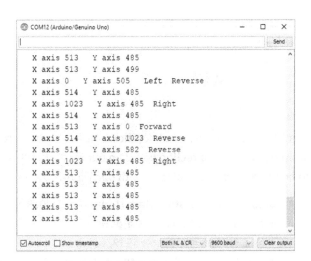

Using two DC geared Hobby Motors requires an H-Bridge and a little more knowledge of the Arduino's PWM. The PWM pins for the Uno are 3, 5, 6, 9, 10 and 11. Pins 3, 5,10 and 11 are 490Hz. Pins 6 and 9 are 980Hz. We will use the Serial Monitor to send commands to your robot. The enable motors can be any of the digital pins. Eventually we want this robot to run without the PC after we have it working well on the bench. Depending on your motors an external battery maybe required. We are using the 9.5V 2000 mAh battery. The battery positive connects to the **H-bridge** Pin 8 and the ground to the negative rail of the breadboard. Using the external power source can damage your Arduino, be very careful.

```
/* Arduino_2DC_Motors with serial input Herb Norbom 10/30/2019
 * use serial monitor for input motor commands
*/
#define Left1  10       // H-bridge (pin 10)
#define Left2  3        // H-bridge (pin 15)
#define Right1  5       // H-bridge (pin 2)
#define Right2  11      // H-bridge (pin 7)
#define enableMotor 12  // enable H-Bridge(pin 1 and 9)
int speedLT = 215;
int speedRT = 215;
char inChar =0;
int maxSpeed=255;
int onTimer(300);

void setup() {
  Serial.begin(9600);
  pinMode(Left1, OUTPUT); // set the pins as outputs, with power off:
  pinMode(Left2, OUTPUT);
  pinMode(Right1, OUTPUT);
  pinMode(Right2, OUTPUT);
  digitalWrite(Left1, LOW);
  digitalWrite(Left2, LOW);
  digitalWrite(Right1, LOW);
  digitalWrite(Right2, LOW);
  pinMode(enableMotor, OUTPUT);
  digitalWrite(enableMotor, LOW);
  Serial.println("Ready...");
  Serial.println("Press letter 'e' to enable H-Bridge");
}
void loop(){
```

```
if ( Serial.available()>0){
  inChar = Serial.read();
  Serial.println(inChar);
  if (inChar == 'e')      //enable H-Bridge
    {digitalWrite(enableMotor, HIGH);  // enable H-bridge high
    Serial.println("Motors enabled");}
  if (inChar == 'd')      //disable H-Bridge
    {digitalWrite(enableMotor, LOW);  // disable H-bridge LOW
    Serial.println("Motors disabled");}
  if (inChar == '2')      //Reverse
    {stRev();}
  else if (inChar == '5')  //stop
    {allStop();}
  else if (inChar == '8')  //forward
    {stFwd();}
  else if (inChar == '4')  //turn Left
    {tLeft();}
  else if (inChar == '6')  //turn Right
    {tRight();}
  else if (inChar == 'a')  //increase Speed Right Motor
  {if (speedRT < maxSpeed-2)
    {speedRT +=2;
     DisplayInfo();
     delay(5);}}      //in milliseconds 1000 in a second
  else if (inChar == 'w')  //increase Speed Left Motor
  {if (speedLT < maxSpeed-2)
    {speedLT +=2;
     DisplayInfo();
     delay(5);}}      //in milliseconds 1000 in a second
  else if (inChar == 'z')   //decrease Speed Right
  {if (speedRT > 0)
    {speedRT -=2;
     DisplayInfo();
     delay(5);}}      //in milliseconds 1000 in a second
  else if (inChar == 'h')    //decrease Speed Left
  {if (speedLT > 0)
    {speedLT -=2;
     DisplayInfo();
```

```
        delay(5);}}      //in milliseconds 1000 in a second
  }
}

void DisplayInfo(){
    Serial.println("LEFT RIGHT");
    Serial.print(speedLT);
    Serial.print("  ");
    Serial.println(speedRT);
}
void allStop(){
  digitalWrite(Left1, LOW);
  digitalWrite(Left2, LOW);
  digitalWrite(Right1, LOW);
  digitalWrite(Right2, LOW);
}
void tRight(){
  digitalWrite(Left2, HIGH);
  digitalWrite(Left1, LOW);
  digitalWrite(Right1, LOW);
  digitalWrite(Right2, HIGH);
  analogWrite(Left2, maxSpeed);
  analogWrite(Right2, maxSpeed);
  delay(onTimer);
  digitalWrite(Left2, LOW);
  digitalWrite(Right2, LOW);
}
void tLeft(){
  digitalWrite(Left1, HIGH);
  digitalWrite(Left2, LOW);
  digitalWrite(Right2, LOW);
  digitalWrite(Right1, HIGH);
  analogWrite(Left1, maxSpeed);
  analogWrite(Right1, maxSpeed);
  delay(onTimer);
  digitalWrite(Left1, LOW);
  digitalWrite(Right1, LOW);
}
```

```
void stFwd(){
  digitalWrite(Left1, LOW);
  digitalWrite(Left2, HIGH);
  digitalWrite(Right1, HIGH);
  digitalWrite(Right2, LOW);
  analogWrite(Left2, speedLT);
  analogWrite(Right1, speedRT);
  delay(onTimer);
  digitalWrite(Left2, LOW);
  digitalWrite(Right1, LOW);
}
void stRev(){
  digitalWrite(Left2, LOW);
  digitalWrite(Left1, HIGH);
  digitalWrite(Right2, HIGH);
  digitalWrite(Right1, LOW);
  analogWrite(Left1, speedLT);
  analogWrite(Right2, speedRT);
  delay(onTimer);
  digitalWrite(Left1, LOW);
  digitalWrite(Right2, LOW);
}
```

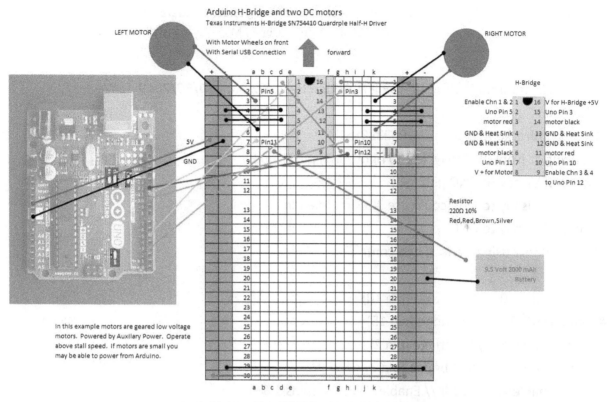

Arduino H-Bridge and two DC motors
Texas Instruments H-Bridge SN754410 Quardrple Half-H Driver

LEFT MOTOR   RIGHT MOTOR

With Motor Wheels on front
With Serial USB Connection   forward

H-Bridge

Enable Chn 1 & 2	1	16	V for H-Bridge +5V
Uno Pin 5	2	15	Uno Pin 3
motor red	3	14	motor black
GND & Heat Sink	4	13	GND & Heat Sink
GND & Heat Sink	5	12	GND & Heat Sink
motor black	6	11	motor red
Uno Pin 11	7	10	Uno Pin 10
V + for Motor	8	9	Enable Chn 3 & 4
			to Uno Pin 12

Resistor
220Ω 10%
Red,Red,Brown,Silver

9.5 Volt 2000 mAh
Battery

In this example motors are geared low voltage
motors. Powered by Auxilary Power. Operate
above stall speed. If motors are small you
may be able to power from Arduino.

C:\Users\Herb\Documents\BOOKSpublish\Arduino Projects\[ArduinoProjects.xlsx]2DC_H_Bridge

```
COM6                                    —    □    ×
|                                          Send
Ready...
Press letter 'e' to enable H-Bridge
e
Motors enabled
8
2
4
6
a
LEFT RIGHT
215   217
d
Motors disabled

Autoscroll  Show timestamp    No line ending  9600 baud   Clear output
```

Project 19 Robot Infrared Control

Using a Roku TV remote to control a robot, but any can work. Two small geared DC motors with an H-Bridge. Communicate using the remote and an Infrared Receiver. While getting the program to work use the Serial Monitor to see the signals received. Change the codes as needed to work with your transmitter. After you have everything working you can disconnect the Serial Cable and control the robot with your remote. The DC motors are powered from the External Battery. The Arduino is also powered by the same battery. A small resistor is useful to pull the H-Bridge enable pins to ground. Once you are ready to run use a battery to power the Uno. We used a 9.6V battery to power all. When you are testing if the motors will not run you may need to use an external power supply in addition

to the USB connection. This project does require a download from git hub. Software is free at
https://github.com/z3t0/Arduino-IRremote. Use the Arduino Library Manager to install the software.

/* Arduino_Remote_Robot_IR using H-Bridge Herb Norbom 10/30/2019

```
 * for Roku Remote
 * Vishay Infrared Receiver  TSOP32338SS1V
 * looking at front of Vishay, left to right(pin1, pin2, pin3)
 * pin 1 of Vishay to UNO pin2
 * pin 2 of Vishay to +5V (could use 3.3V)middle Pin
 * pin 3 of Vishay to GND
 * 2 DC motors using PWM speed control
 */
#define Left1  10    // H-bridge (pin 10)
#define Left2  3     // H-bridge (pin 15)
#define Right1  5    // H-bridge (pin 2)
#define Right2  11   // H-bridge (pin 7)
#define enableMotor 12    // Enable H-Bridge (pins 1 & 9)
int speedLT = 240;      // this speed when running from battery 150 from USB 190
int speedRT = 240;
int runTime = 400;

#include <IRremote.h>
const int RECV_PIN = 2;
IRrecv irrecv(RECV_PIN);
decode_results results;

void setup()
{
  Serial.begin(9600);
  irrecv.enableIRIn(); // Start the receiver
  Serial.println("Enabled IRin");
  Serial.print("Starting...\n");
  pinMode(Left1, OUTPUT);  // set all the pins you're using as outputs, with power off:
  pinMode(Left2, OUTPUT);
  pinMode(Right1, OUTPUT);
  pinMode(Right2, OUTPUT);
  digitalWrite(Left1, LOW);
  digitalWrite(Left2, LOW);
```

```
digitalWrite(Right1, LOW);
digitalWrite(Right2, LOW);
analogWrite(Left2,speedLT);
analogWrite(Right2,speedRT);
analogWrite(Left1,speedLT);
analogWrite(Right1,speedRT);
pinMode(enableMotor, OUTPUT);
digitalWrite(enableMotor, LOW); //keep motors off
}
/*              OLDER           NEWER
 *              Roku codes      Roku codes     Sceptre Codes
 * up arrow    1464047719  forward    3475889595    752
 *right arrow  1464054859  right turn 2270865887    3280
 *down arrow  1464060979  reverse    3967014751    2800
 *left arrow   1464039559  left turn  773990423     720
 *OK           1464030379  stop       282358075     3344(Enter)
 *Note 'stop' really of little use here.  With no threading timer must finish
 *if you see 146030634, 1464047974 or others could be result of holding
 *button too long
 */
void loop() {
 if (irrecv.decode(&results)) {
  Serial.println(results.value);
  if (results.value == 3475889595){//^ UP ARROW
    stFwd();   //straight Fwd, Fwd both motors
  }
  if (results.value == 773990423){//< LEFT ARROW
    tLeft();   // left, right motor Fwd, left motor Rev
  }
  if (results.value == 2270865887){//> RIGHT ARROW
    tRight();  // right, right motor Rev, left motor Fwd
  }
  if (results.value == 3967014751){//DOWN ARROW
    stRev();   //straight Rev, Rev both motors
  }
  if (results.value == 2842358075){//SELECT or OK
    allStop();
  }
```

```arduino
   irrecv.resume(); // Receive the next value
 }
 delay(100);
}
void allStop(){
 Serial.println("STOP called");
 digitalWrite(enableMotor, LOW); // de-enable H-bridge pins 1 & 9
 digitalWrite(Left1, LOW);
 digitalWrite(Left2, LOW);
 digitalWrite(Right1, LOW);
 digitalWrite(Right2, LOW);
}
void tRight(){
 Serial.println("RIGHT TURN");
 digitalWrite(Left2, HIGH);
 digitalWrite(Left1, LOW);
 digitalWrite(Right1, LOW);
 digitalWrite(Right2, HIGH);
 digitalWrite(enableMotor, HIGH);  // enable H-bridge pins 1 & 9
 delay(runTime);
 allStop();
}
void tLeft(){
 Serial.println("LEFT TURN");
 digitalWrite(Left1, HIGH);
 digitalWrite(Left2, LOW);
 digitalWrite(Right2, LOW);
 digitalWrite(Right1, HIGH);
 digitalWrite(enableMotor, HIGH);  // enable H-bridge pins 1 & 9
 delay(runTime);
 allStop();
}
void stFwd(){
 Serial.println("FORWARD");
 digitalWrite(Left1, LOW);
 digitalWrite(Left2, HIGH);
 digitalWrite(Right1, HIGH);
 digitalWrite(Right2, LOW);
```

```
digitalWrite(enableMotor, HIGH);  // enable H-bridge pins 1 & 9
 delay(runTime);
 allStop();
}
void stRev(){
 Serial.println("REVERSE");
 digitalWrite(Left2, LOW);
 digitalWrite(Left1, HIGH);
 digitalWrite(Right2, HIGH);
 digitalWrite(Right1, LOW);
 digitalWrite(enableMotor, HIGH);  // enable H-bridge pins 1 & 9
 delay(runTime);
 allStop();
}
```

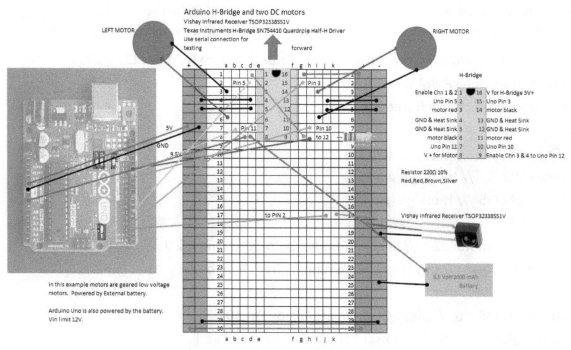

Battery with homemade adapter

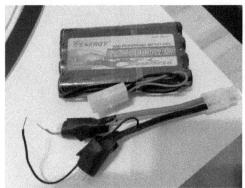

```
2842358075
STOP called
3475889595
FORWARD
STOP called
3967014751
REVERSE
STOP called
2270865887
RIGHT TURN
STOP called
773990423
LEFT TURN
STOP called
2842358075
STOP called
```

Project 19 two DC Motors Follow Line

Build on the previous example. Add two-Infrared Sensors (Obstacle Avoidance or line follow). You may need to change rotation of wheels as we want the Infrared Sensors on the front of the robot. You may need to shield sensors if having a problem. Many sensors have a potentiometer for adjustment, which is handy. This program is to follow a black tape line. We have left in the output to the serial monitor as this will help you tune your sensors.

```
/* Arduino_2DC_Motors_Stay_On_Line using H-Bridge Herb Norbom 11/2/2019
 * 2 DC motors using PWM speed control
 * 2 Obstacle Detection Infrared Sensors
 */
#define Left1  10   // H-bridge (pin 10)
#define Left2  3    // H-bridge (pin 15)
#define Right1  5   // H-bridge (pin 2)
#define Right2  11  // H-bridge (pin 7)
#define enableMotor 12    // Enable H-Bridge both sides pins 1 & 9
int speedLT = 70;     // this speed when running from 9.5V battery 70
int speedRT = 70;
const int RightA0 = 0;  //Edge Sensor Right, Analog Pin A0
const int LeftA1 = 1;   //Edge Sensor Left, Analog Pin A1
int RightReading = 0;   //variable Reading A0 Infrared Sensor
int LeftReading = 0;    //variable Reading A1 Infrared Sensor
void setup()
{
  Serial.begin(9600);
  pinMode(Left1, OUTPUT);  // set all the pins you're using as outputs, with power off:
  pinMode(Left2, OUTPUT);
  pinMode(Right1, OUTPUT);
  pinMode(Right2, OUTPUT);
```

```
    digitalWrite(Left1, LOW);
    digitalWrite(Left2, LOW);
    digitalWrite(Right1, LOW);
    digitalWrite(Right2, LOW);
    analogWrite(Left2,speedLT);
    analogWrite(Right2,speedRT);
    analogWrite(Left1,speedLT);
    analogWrite(Right1,speedRT);
    pinMode(enableMotor, OUTPUT);
    digitalWrite(enableMotor, LOW); //keep motors off
    Serial.print("Starting in 5 seconds...\n");
    delay(5000);          //approx 5 seconds to give you time to set up
}

void loop() {
  CheckSensors();          //Review Infrared sensors
  delay(50);
  if (RightReading > 550){
    allStop();
    tLeft();
  }
  else if (LeftReading > 550){
    allStop();
    tRight();
  }
  else {
    stFwd();
    allStop();}
}
void allStop(){
  digitalWrite(enableMotor, LOW); // de-enable H-bridge pins 1 & 9
  delay(15);
// digitalWrite(Left1, LOW);    // Left in as you may need if not using enable
// digitalWrite(Left2, LOW);
// digitalWrite(Right1, LOW);
// digitalWrite(Right2, LOW);
  }
void tRight(){
```

```
    Serial.println("RIGHT turn");
    digitalWrite(Left2, HIGH);
    digitalWrite(Left1, LOW);
    digitalWrite(Right1, HIGH);
    digitalWrite(Right2, LOW);
    digitalWrite(enableMotor, HIGH);  // enable H-bridge pins 1 & 9
    delay(50);
    allStop();
}
void tLeft(){
    Serial.println("LEFT turn");
    digitalWrite(Left1, HIGH);
    digitalWrite(Left2, LOW);
    digitalWrite(Right2, HIGH);
    digitalWrite(Right1, LOW);
    digitalWrite(enableMotor, HIGH);  // enable H-bridge pins 1 & 9
    delay(50);
    allStop();
}
void stFwd(){
    Serial.println("STRAIGHT FWD");
    digitalWrite(Left1, LOW);
    digitalWrite(Left2, HIGH);
    digitalWrite(Right1, LOW);
    digitalWrite(Right2, HIGH);
    digitalWrite(enableMotor, HIGH);  // enable H-bridge pins 1 & 9
    delay(20);
    allStop();
}

void CheckSensors(){
    RightReading = analogRead(RightA0);
    Serial.print("        Right:  "); //left in for testing
    Serial.print(RightReading);
    Serial.print("  Left:  ");
    LeftReading = analogRead(LeftA1);
    Serial.println(LeftReading);
}
```

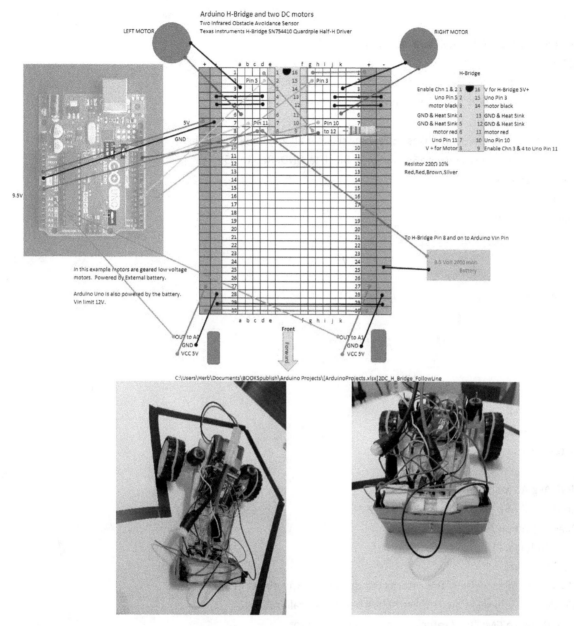

Project 20 Sharp Infrared Distance Sensor

We found our sensor to be accurate within 1 – 2 inches. The sensor range is reported to be 20cm to 150cm (7.8in to 59in). When testing be aware that the sensor uses a narrow beam. The "SharpIR" library needs to be added.

Our program includes a display of the raw analog reading, the associated voltage and distances (cm, in, feet).

```
//Arduino_Sharp_Infrared_Sensor Herb Norbom 4/11/2019
// infraredSensor  Sharp 2YOA02
// model: integer that determines your sensor:  1080 for GP2Y0A21Y
//                        20150 for GP2Y0A02Y
// measure to base of Sensor.
#include <SharpIR.h>   // this script takes 25 reading from analog pin, median return as cm
#define ir A0         // In our case White Sensor wire, Black to GND, Red to +5V
#define model 20150
int tempR = 0;
SharpIR SharpIR(ir, model);

void setup() {
  Serial.begin(9600);
  Serial.println("...Ready...");
}

void loop() {
  delay(2000);
  tempR =0;
  for (int x =0;x<5;x++){
    tempR = analogRead(ir);
    tempR = tempR + tempR;
  }
  Serial.print("Avg A0 readings: ");
  Serial.print(tempR / 5);
  float voltage  = (tempR /5)*(5.0 /1023.0);
  Serial.print(" Voltage: ");
  Serial.println(voltage);
  int disCM=SharpIR.distance(); // this returns the distance to the object in CM
  disCM= disCM + 0; //do slight adjustment here if needed to calibrate
  Serial.print("Distance CM: ");  // returns it to the serial monitor
  Serial.print(disCM);

  float disIN = disCM*0.393701;
  Serial.print("   INCHES: ");  // returns it to the serial monitor
  Serial.print(disIN,1);      // print with one decimal position
  Serial.print("   FEET: ");  // returns it to the serial monitor
  float disFEET = disIN/12.0;
  Serial.println(disFEET,1);  // print with one decimal position
}
```

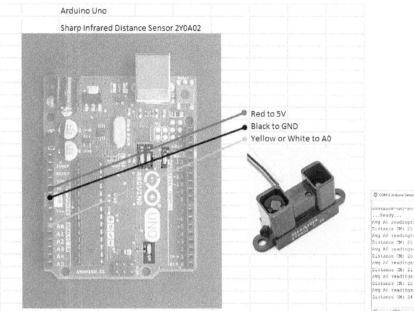

Arduino Uno

Sharp Infrared Distance Sensor 2Y0A02

Red to 5V
Black to GND
Yellow or White to A0

Project 21 Servo

A simple Tower Pro SG90 Micro Servo is used. Use the Arduino Servo library. If you have multiple servos you will want to obtain a servo hat. These hats can support multiple servos and provide external power. As we are using a micro servo with low amperage needs, we will power via the Arduino. Be sure not to let the servo stall or it could damage the Arduino.

```
/* Arduino_Servo Herb Norbom 4/15/2019
 Test the range of a servo using the Arduino library for servos.
 Displays the position of the servo. Will complete two sweeps
 of the range. Using a micro servo 180 degree sweep.
 You can also enter the desired position after the sweeps are completed.
*/

#include <Servo.h>
int count =0;      // variable to count loops
Servo myservo;     // create servo object to control a servo
int pos = 0;       // variable to store the servo position
```

```
String inputString="";
boolean stringComplete = false;
int posWanted = 0;  // variable for Serial Input position of servo

void setup() {
  Serial.begin(9600);
  Serial.print("Starting...\n");
  myservo.attach(9);  // attaches the servo on pin 9 to the servo object
}

void loop() {
  if (stringComplete){
    Serial.print("Input: ");
    Serial.println(inputString);
    posWanted = inputString.toInt();     //convert string to integer
    stringComplete = false;
    inputString="";
    if (posWanted >=0 && posWanted <=180){
      myservo.write(posWanted);          // servo to position
      Serial.println("Enter Desired Servo Postion from 0 to 180: ");
    }
  }
  while (count <2){
    for (pos = 0; pos <= 180; pos += 1) { // from 0 degrees to 180 degrees, in 1 degree steps
      myservo.write(pos);          // tell servo to go to position in variable 'pos'
      Serial.println(pos);
      delay(30);                   // waits 30ms for the servo to reach the position
    }
    delay(200);
    for (pos = 180; pos >= 0; pos -= 1) {
      myservo.write(pos);
      Serial.println(pos);
      delay(30);
    }
    count +=1;
    delay(200);
    if (count == 2){
    Serial.println("Enter Desired Servo Position from 0 to 180: ");
    }
  }
}

void serialEvent() {
  while (Serial.available()) {
    char inChar = (char)Serial.read();     // get the new byte
```

```
  inputString += inChar;           // add it to the inputString
  // if the incoming character is a newline, set a flag
  if (inChar == '\n') {
    stringComplete = true;
  }
 }
}
```

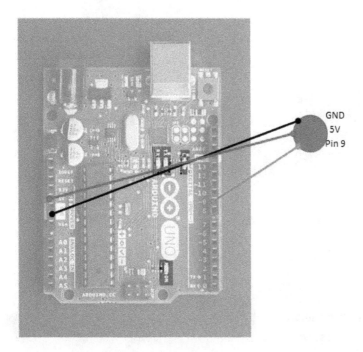

Arduino
Tower Pro SG90 Micro Servo

GND
5V
Pin 9

Caution: If you are using servos that draw
current in excess of Arduino capacity you should
use an H-Bridge or a servo hat with external power.

Working with Continuous Rotation Servos

We are using micro servos, FEETECH FSR90R 360° Rotation Continuous Servo to keep amperage to a lower level. We are going to do three projects that demonstrate using the servos in robots. The first project we will use the Serial Monitor to send commands for controlling the robot. With these continuous servos a pulse of '90' is neutral or no movement. A pulse from 91 to 180 is clockwise and from 1 to 89 is counterclockwise when using Arduino <Servo.h>.

Project 22 Testing two continuous servos

/* Arduino_Two_Contin_Rot_Servos Herb Norbom 4/12/2019
  two continuous micro servos. Run from Arduino. Avoid stalls
  possible damage to Arduino. Object of this program is to get servos working.
  Use Serial Monitor to communicate to Arduino
*/

```
#include <Servo.h>
Servo myservoLT;   // create servo object to control a servo
Servo myservoRT;
char inChar = 0;   // for Serial input
void setup() {
  Serial.begin(9600);
  Serial.print("Starting...\n");
}

void loop() {
  if ( Serial.available() > 0) {
   inChar = Serial.read();
   if (inChar == '2') {stRev();}
   else if (inChar == '5'){allStop();}    //stop
   else if (inChar == '8'){stFwd();}      //forward
   else if (inChar == '4'){tLeft();}      //turn Left
   else if (inChar == '6'){tRight();}     //turn Right
  }
}
void allStop() {
  myservoRT.detach(); //detach servo to prevent "creeping" effect
  myservoLT.detach();
}
void tLeft() {
  Serial.println(" Turn Left ");
  myservoRT.attach(3);  //attach servo to pin 3 Right servo
  myservoLT.attach(9);  //attach servo to pin 9 Left servo
  myservoRT.write(0);
  myservoLT.write(0);
  delay(200); //rotation duration in ms
  allStop();
}

void tRight() {
  Serial.println(" Turn Right ");
  myservoRT.attach(3);
  myservoLT.attach(9);
  myservoRT.write(180);
  myservoLT.write(180);
  delay(200);
  allStop();
}
void stFwd() {
  Serial.println(" FORWARD ");
  myservoRT.attach(3);
```

```
  myservoLT.attach(9);
  myservoRT.write(180);
  myservoLT.write(0);
  delay(500);
  allStop();
}
void stRev() {
  Serial.println(" REVERSE ");
  myservoRT.attach(3);
  myservoLT.attach(9);
  myservoRT.write(0);
  myservoLT.write(180);
  delay(500);
  allStop();
}
```

Arduino   with two continious micro servos

FEETECH FSR90R 360° Rotation Continuous Servo

Caution: If you are using servos that draw
current in excess of Arduino capacity you should
use an H-Bridge or a servo hat with external power.

Project 23 Stay in the Ring

With this project we have added two infrared sensors. Mounted on the front of your robot and approximately ¼" above the surface. We made a ring using white cardboard (28"x22") and added a black circle (9" to 10" radius) using electrical tape. Depending on the infrared sensors you select you may need to adjust program values. The lighting in the room can cause problems, shield the sensors if having problems. The objective of the program is to stay within the ring. As the robot will need to run independent of the Serial Monitor you will need external power. We suggest a 9.6V 2000 mAh battery with a switch and plug.

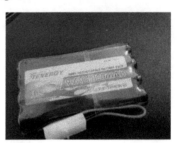

```
/* Arduino_Stay _In_Ring_Servos  Herb Norbom 4/13/2019
    two continuous micro servos.  Run from Arduino. Avoid stalls
    possible damage to Arduino.  Use two infrared detectors to stay within
    black boundaries.  Serial input controls left in for testing purposes.
    Robot will start moving within 5 seconds of program load. Be ready
    to catch it.
*/
#include <Servo.h>
Servo myservoLT;     // create servo object to control a servo
Servo myservoRT;     // create servo object to control a servo

char inChar =0;     // for Serial input
const int RightA0 = 0;  //Edge Sensor Front Right, Analog Pin A0
const int LeftA1 = 1;   //Edge Sensor Front Left, Analog Pin A1
int RightReading = 0;   //variable Reading A0 Infrared Sensor
int LeftReading = 0;    //variable Reading A1 Infrared Sensor

void setup() {
  Serial.begin(9600);
  Serial.print("Starting...\n");
  delay(5000);//approx 5 seconds to give you time to set up
}

void loop() {
  CheckSensors(); //Review all input sensors for fresh data
  if (RightReading > 900){
//    Serial.println("Right EDGE found");
    allStop();
    stRev();
    tLeft();
    stFwd();
```

```
  }
  if (LeftReading > 900){
//   Serial.println("Left EDGE found");
    allStop();
    stRev();
    tRight();
    stFwd();
  }

  if ( Serial.available()>0){
   inChar = Serial.read();
   if (inChar == '2') {stRev();}        //reverse
   else if (inChar == '5'){allStop();} //stop
   else if (inChar == '8'){stFwd();}    //forward
   else if (inChar == '4'){tLeft();}    //turn Left
   else if (inChar == '6'){tRight();}   //turn Right
  }
  stFwd();
}
void allStop(){
  myservoRT.detach(); //detach servo to prevent "creeping" effect
  myservoLT.detach(); //detach servo to prevent "creeping" effect
}
void tLeft(){
//  Serial.println(" Turn Left ");
  myservoRT.attach(3); //reattach servo to pin 3
  myservoLT.attach(9);  // attaches the servo on pin 9 to the LEFT servo
  myservoRT.write(65);
  myservoLT.write(65);
  delay(400); //rotation duration in ms
  allStop();
}

void tRight(){
//  Serial.println(" Turn Right ");
  myservoRT.attach(3); //reattach servo to pin 3
  myservoLT.attach(9);  // attaches the servo on pin 9 to the LEFT servo
  myservoRT.write(150);
  myservoLT.write(150);
  delay(400); //rotation duration in ms
  allStop();
}
void stFwd(){
//  Serial.println(" FORWARD ");
  myservoRT.attach(3); //reattach servo to pin 3
```

```
myservoLT.attach(9);  // attaches the servo on pin 9 to the LEFT servo
myservoRT.write(130);
myservoLT.write(50);
delay(100); //rotation duration in ms
allStop();
}
void stRev(){
// Serial.println(" REVERSE ");
myservoRT.attach(3); //reattach servo to pin 3
myservoLT.attach(9);  // attaches the servo on pin 9 to the LEFT servo
myservoRT.write(65);
myservoLT.write(130);
delay(500); //rotation duration in ms
allStop();
}


void CheckSensors(){
RightReading = analogRead(RightA0);
// Serial.print("A0 Right ");
// Serial.print(RightReading);
LeftReading = analogRead(LeftA1);
// Serial.print("   A1 Left ");
// Serial.println(LeftReading);
}
```

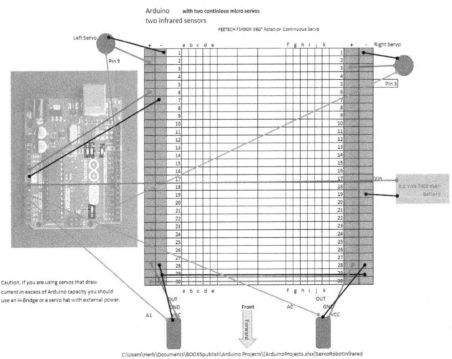

Project 24 Attack Object in the Ring

Building on what we achieved in previous programs. Place your robot in the ring it will turn LEFT until it detects object (block of wood). Charge the object and push it out of the ring. Movement will start in five seconds, be ready to catch robot.

```
/* Arduino_Servo_Attack  Herb Norbom 4/16/2019
   two continuous micro servos.  Run from Arduino. Avoid stalls
   possible damage to Arduino.  With Ultra-Sonic Sensor detect object and attack.
   Use two infrared detectors to stay within black boundaries.
   Serial input controls left for testing purposes.
   Robot will start moving within 5 seconds of program load. Be ready
   to catch it.
*/
#include <Servo.h>
Servo myservoLT;        // create servo object to control servo
Servo myservoRT;
#define echoPin  8      // Echo Pin Ultra-Sonic
#define trigPin  7      // Trigger Pin Ultra-Sonic
long Duration;
float Distance_in;      // use float want decimals for distance
const int RightA0 = 0;  //Edge Sensor Front Right, Analog Pin A0
const int LeftA1 = 1;   //Edge Sensor Front Left, Analog Pin A1
int RightReading = 0;   //variable Reading A0 Infrared Sensor
int LeftReading = 0;    //variable Reading A1 Infrared Sensor

void setup() {
  Serial.begin(9600);
  pinMode(trigPin, OUTPUT); //ultrasonic sensor trigger pin output.
  pinMode(echoPin, INPUT);  //ultrasonic sensor echo pin as an input.
  Serial.print("Starting in 5 seconds...\n");
  delay(5000);            //approx 5 seconds to give you time to set up
}

void loop(){
  CheckSensors();         //Review Infrared sensors
  if (RightReading > 900){
    allStop();
    stRev();
    tLeft();
    stFwd();
  }
  if (LeftReading > 900){
    allStop();
    stRev();
    tRight();
    stFwd();
```

```
    }
  UltraSensed();
  if (Distance_in <11.4){
    stFwd();}
  else if(Distance_in >=11.4){ tLeft();
  }
  delay(150);
}
void allStop(){
  myservoRT.detach();   //detach servo to prevent "creeping" effect
  myservoLT.detach();
}
void tLeft(){
  myservoRT.attach(3);  //attach servo to pin 3
  myservoLT.attach(9);  //attach servo on pin 9
  myservoRT.write(65);
  myservoLT.write(65);
  delay(500); //rotation duration in ms
  allStop();
}

void tRight(){
  myservoRT.attach(3);
  myservoLT.attach(9);
  myservoRT.write(150);
  myservoLT.write(150);
  delay(400);
  allStop();
}
void stFwd(){
  myservoRT.attach(3);
  myservoLT.attach(9);
  myservoRT.write(130);
  myservoLT.write(50);
  delay(200);
  allStop();
}
void stRev(){
  myservoRT.attach(3);
  myservoLT.attach(9);
  myservoRT.write(65);
  myservoLT.write(130);
  delay(500);
  allStop();
}
```

```
void UltraSensed(){
 digitalWrite(trigPin, LOW);   // Clear or off trigPin
 delayMicroseconds(2);
 digitalWrite(trigPin, HIGH);  // Set trigPin to HIGH for 10 micro seconds
 delayMicroseconds(10);
 digitalWrite(trigPin, LOW);
 Duration = pulseIn(echoPin, HIGH); // Read the echoPin, returns the sound wave travel time microseconds
 Distance_in = Duration * 0.01351221/2;
 Serial.println(Distance_in, 1);
 }
void CheckSensors(){
 RightReading = analogRead(RightA0);
 LeftReading = analogRead(LeftA1);
}
```

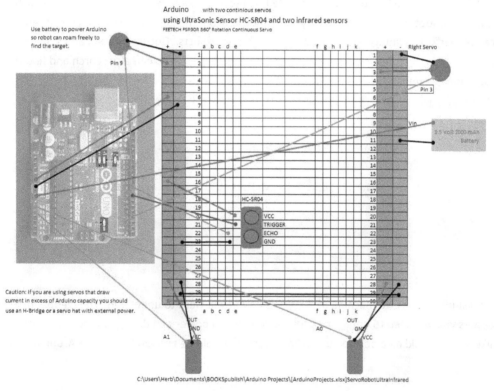

Stepper Motors

When you want more precise movement than you can get with a regular DC motor you have two basic choices, servo and stepper motors. Stepper motors can be very precise, they require a little more knowledge to use vs other motors. There are various types, we will just look at the more standard ones; 2-phase bipolar and 4-phase unipolar. Of course, there are many sizes with different torque ratings. You also need to think of the step count. That is the number of steps to make one complete revolution. Like other motors there are geared stepper motors. With gears the torque can be increased as well as the steps per revolution, giving it more torque and precision. Adafruit has put together a great summary at https://learn.adafruit.com/all-about-stepper-motors/types-of-steppers. Another good source is from Tom Igoe http://www.tigoe.com/pcomp/code/circuits/motors/stepper-motors/.

The Arduino IDE comes with a Stepper library included and several examples. We have found the <AccelStepper.h> library to be a little smoother. Install the library as with other from the 'Sketch\Include Library\Manage Libraries' type in "accelstepper". This library will be used in some of our projects. Documentation and some examples are available at http://www.airspayce.com/mikem/arduino/AccelStepper/. You can also search and find the zip file to install. For additional commands see
http://www.airspayce.com/mikem/arduino/AccelStepper/classAccelStepper.html

If your project list includes a CNC machine or a 3D printer you will want to understand the stepper motors. With multiple steppers you will need to obtain a motor shield that can power and drive your steppers. Steppers can hold a position, like servos. Holding a position does draw current. Could be enough to damage Arduino, be careful.

Project 25 Single Stepper 28BYJ 48 Unipolar

For our first stepper project we will use the "accelstepper" library and a small 5V inexpensive unipolar stepper that is widely available. For example, on Amazon a set of 5 with the ULN2003 Driver board for the Arduino is from $12 to $14. The Driver boards being are inexpensive and easy to use. Specifications call for 5.625 step angle degrees for 64 steps (360/5.625 = 64). One revolution 4,096 steps (5.624/64=.087875) and (360 / .087875 = 4,096.73. With this gearing the stepper will be a little off with each revolution as number of steps must be an integer. In our example program you can input position to move to (number of steps). One revolution (when looking down on servo) clockwise is approximately -4,096, for counterclockwise enter 4,096. To return to start position enter 0. For ¼ turn (90° counterclockwise)00 enter 1,024. All positions are reference from start position of 0. If we said move 100 and then 150 the servo would first move 100 steps and then 50 steps. We are sure you can see how precise this little stepper can be. The program also provides for setting acceleration, maximum speed and speed. Speed did not seem to change as values were given for this stepper, but using Maximum Speed achieved the desired result. Acceleration works well, stepper barely turns at 5.

```
/* Arduino_AccelStepper28BYJ_48  4/20/2019  Herb Norbom
 * single stepper with variable inputs to control speed, position and acceleration
 * When powered up where stepper is becomes position 0
 * Your moves are in reference to that position 0, multiple moves adjust based on position 0
 * Enter 0 to return to start or 'h' to reset servo to zero
 * As setup to test position, speed and acceleration precede each input with p,s,a
 */
#include <AccelStepper.h>
#define HALFSTEP 8 //was 8

// Motor pin definitions
#define motorPin1 8    // IN1 on the ULN2003 driver 1
#define motorPin2 9    // IN2 on the ULN2003 driver 1
#define motorPin3 10   // IN3 on the ULN2003 driver 1
#define motorPin4 11   // IN4 on the ULN2003 driver 1

// Initialize with pin sequence IN1-IN3-IN2-IN4 for using the AccelStepper with 28BYJ-48
AccelStepper stepper28BYJ_48(HALFSTEP, motorPin1, motorPin3, motorPin2, motorPin4);

String inputString="";
boolean stringComplete = false;
String temp ="";
int tempI = 0;
float tempF =0.0;
float MaxSpeed=1000.0;
float Acceleration = 700.0;
int Speed = 800;

void setup() {
  Serial.begin(9600);
  Serial.println("For position enter p + integer");
  Serial.print("For maximum speed enter m + integer. Current= ");
  Serial.println(MaxSpeed);
  Serial.print("For Acceleration enter a + float or integer. Current=  ");
  Serial.println(Acceleration);
  Serial.print("For Speed enter s + integer. Current=  ");
  Serial.println(Speed);
  Serial.println("For two revolutions enter f  ");
  Serial.println("Reset Servo to position 0   enter h  ");
  Serial.println("Ready...");

  inputString.reserve(20);
```

```
    stepper28BYJ_48.setMaxSpeed(MaxSpeed);    //default 1000.0, 10 very slow to 1000 can be integer
    stepper28BYJ_48.setAcceleration(Acceleration); //default  700.0
    stepper28BYJ_48.setSpeed(Speed);          //default 800 doesn't appear to work with this stepper
}

void loop() {
  if (stringComplete){
    Serial.print("Starting Position: ");
    Serial.println(stepper28BYJ_48.currentPosition());
    Serial.print("Value entered: ");
    Serial.println(inputString);

    int len = inputString.length();
    if (inputString[0] == 'p'){         //move to position
      for (int x =1;x <len;x++){
        temp = temp+ inputString[x];
      }
      tempI = temp.toInt();
      stepper28BYJ_48.moveTo(tempI);
    }
    if (inputString[0] == 'm'){         //set maxmium speed
      for (int x =1;x <len;x++){
        temp = temp+ inputString[x];
      }
      tempF = temp.toFloat();
      MaxSpeed = tempF;
      stepper28BYJ_48.setMaxSpeed(MaxSpeed);
    }
    if (inputString[0] == 'a'){         //set Acceleration
      for (int x =1;x <len;x++){
        temp = temp+ inputString[x];
      }
      tempF = temp.toFloat();
      Acceleration = tempF;
      stepper28BYJ_48.setAcceleration(Acceleration);
    }
    if (inputString[0] == 's'){         //set Speed
      for (int x =1;x <len;x++){
        temp = temp+ inputString[x];
      }
      tempI = temp.toInt();
      Speed = tempI;
      stepper28BYJ_48.setSpeed(Speed);
      Serial.print("Starting Speed: ");
      Serial.println(stepper28BYJ_48.speed());
```

```arduino
    }
    if (inputString[0] == 'f'){          //forward two revolutions
      stepper28BYJ_48.moveTo(8192);
    }
    if (inputString[0] == 'h'){          //reset servo to position 0
      stepper28BYJ_48.setCurrentPosition(0);
    }

    inputString="";
    stringComplete = false;
    tempF = 0.0;
    temp="";
    tempI = 0;
  }
  stepper28BYJ_48.run();  // stepper moves based on input
}

void serialEvent() {
  while (Serial.available()) {
    char inChar = (char)Serial.read();     // get the new byte
    inputString += inChar;                 // add it to the inputString
    if (inChar == '\n') {
      stringComplete = true;
    }
  }
}
```

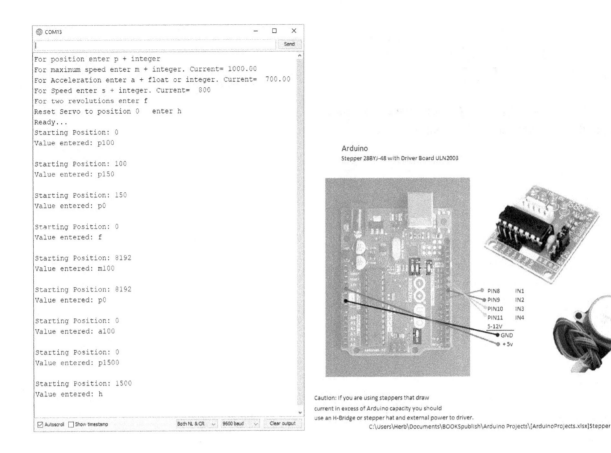

```
COM13                                          —  □  ×

                                                    Send

For position enter p + integer
For maximum speed enter m + integer. Current= 1000.00
For Acceleration enter a + float or integer. Current=  700.00
For Speed enter s + integer. Current=  800
For two revolutions enter f
Reset Servo to position 0   enter h
Ready...
Starting Position: 0
Value entered: p100

Starting Position: 100
Value entered: p150

Starting Position: 150
Value entered: p0

Starting Position: 0
Value entered: f

Starting Position: 8192
Value entered: m100

Starting Position: 8192
Value entered: p0

Starting Position: 0
Value entered: a100

Starting Position: 0
Value entered: p1500

Starting Position: 1500
Value entered: h

☑ Autoscroll  ☐ Show timestamp    Both NL & CR ▾  9600 baud ▾   Clear output
```

Arduino
Stepper 28BYJ-48 with Driver Board ULN2003

PIN8   IN1
PIN9   IN2
PIN10   IN3
PIN11   IN4
5-12V
GND
+ 5v

Caution: If you are using steppers that draw
current in excess of Arduino capacity you should
use an H-Bridge or stepper hat and external power to driver.
C:\Users\Herb\Documents\BOOKSpublish\Arduino Projects\[ArduinoProjects.xlsx]Stepper

Project 26 Bipolar 4 Wire Stepper using <stepper.h>

The stepper was made by ShinanoKenshi and its information is STH-390254 1.8 Deg/Step 60Ω. We are using an H-Bridge and an external power supply. **Do not attempt to power this stepper from the Arduino**. We felt you should see an example using the standard <stepper.h> library included with the Arduino IDE. At 1.8 Deg per step a single revolution will take (360/1.8) = 200 steps. As we are using an H-Bridge we did not need to install and use the AFMotor.h.

```
/* Arduino_stepper_h_library   Herb Norbom 4/20/2019 modified example program of Tom Igoe 2009
 * Stepper 4 wire using H-Bridge
 * Arduino Pin   H-Bridge         BreadBoard
 *     8            2
 *     9            7
 *    10           15
 *    11           10
 *    5V           16            red rail 5V from Arduino
 *    GND          4,5,12,13     blue rail GND from Arduino
 *                 1, 9 enable H-Bridge not used for this project
 *                 8 External +9V, External GND to GND on breadboard
This program drives a bipolar stepper motor.
Stepper is STH-39D254 4 wire 1.8 Deg/Step 60ohm
Speed of 120 is smooth
360/1.8 200 steps per revolution
```

```
    H-Bridge    Stepper    A1=red, A2=yellow, B1=orange, B2=brown
       3           B2       use ohm multimeter to determine pairings
       6           B1       on this stepper wires next to each other pair
      14           A2
      11           A1
*/
#include <Stepper.h>
const int stepsPerRevolution = 200;  // number of steps per revolution
Stepper myStepper(stepsPerRevolution, 8, 9, 10, 11);
String inputString="";
boolean stringComplete = false;
String temp ="";
int tempI = 0;
int Speed = 80;

void setup() {
  myStepper.setSpeed(60);
  Serial.begin(9600);
  Serial.println("Test counter clock wise and clockwise enter t");
  Serial.println("Move counter clock wise number of steps enter p + integer, exp p200 ");
  Serial.println("Move clock wise number of steps enter p - integer, exp p-200 ");
  Serial.print("For Speed enter s + integer 1 to 200, exp s120. Current=  ");
  Serial.println(Speed);
  Serial.println("For two revolutions counter clock wise enter f  ");
  Serial.println("For two revolutions clock wise enter b  ");
  Serial.println("Ready...");
}

void loop() {
  if (stringComplete){
    if (inputString[0] == 't'){ //start testing
      int count = 0;
      while (count < 2){
        Serial.println("clockwise");       //looking at top of stepper
        myStepper.step(-stepsPerRevolution);
        delay(500);
        Serial.println("counter clockwise");
        myStepper.step(stepsPerRevolution);
        delay(500);
        count++;
      }
    }
    int len = inputString.length();
    if (inputString[0] == 'p'){        //move number of steps
      for (int x =1;x <len;x++){
```

```arduino
      temp = temp+ inputString[x];
      }
    templ = temp.toInt();
    myStepper.step(templ);
    }
    if (inputString[0] == 'f'){        //counter clock wise two revolutions
      myStepper.step(stepsPerRevolution*2);
    }
    if (inputString[0] == 'b'){        //clockwise two revolutions
      myStepper.step(-stepsPerRevolution*2);
    }
    if (inputString[0] == 's'){      //set speed
      for (int x =1;x <len;x++){
        temp = temp+ inputString[x];
        }
      templ = temp.toInt();
      if (templ > 0 && templ <= 200){
      Speed = templ;
      myStepper.setSpeed(Speed);
      }
      else {
      Serial.println("Speed out of range, retry between 1 and 200");
      }
      }
    inputString ="";
    stringComplete = false;
    temp="";
    templ = 0;
  }
}
void serialEvent() {
  while (Serial.available()) {
    char inChar = (char)Serial.read();    // get the new byte
    inputString += inChar;          // add it to the inputString
    if (inChar == '\n') {
      stringComplete = true;
      Serial.println(inputString);
    }
  }
}
```

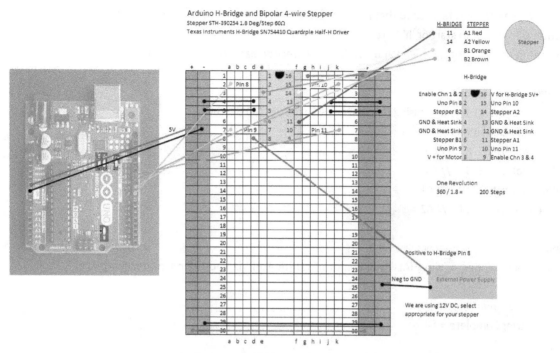

Arduino H-Bridge and Bipolar 4-wire Stepper
Stepper STH-390254 1.8 Deg/Step 60Ω
Texas Instruments H-Bridge SN754410 Quardrple Half-H Driver

H-BRIDGE	STEPPER
11	A1 Red
14	A2 Yellow
6	B1 Orange
3	B2 Brown

H-Bridge

Enable Chn 1 & 2	1	16	V for H-Bridge 5V+
Uno Pin 8	2	15	Uno Pin 10
Stepper B2	3	14	Stepper A2
GND & Heat Sink	4	13	GND & Heat Sink
GND & Heat Sink	5	12	GND & Heat Sink
Stepper B1	6	11	Stepper A1
Uno Pin 9	7	10	Uno Pin 11
V + for Motor	8	9	Enable Chn 3 & 4

One Revolution
360 / 1.8 =   200 Steps

Positive to H-Bridge Pin 8

Neg to GND   External Power Supply

We are using 12V DC, select
appropriate for your stepper

C:\Users\Herb\Documents\BOOKSpublish\Arduino Projects\[ArduinoProjects.xlsx]Stepper_4_Wire_H_Bridge

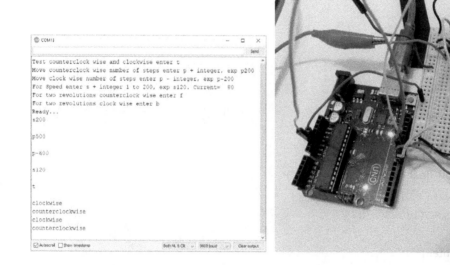

Project 27 4_Wire Stepper using AccelStepper and H-Bridge

Reworking a previous program to use AccelStepper with an H-Bridge and a 4-wire stepper. This is example clearing shows the impact of acceleration and deceleration. **Do not power the stepper from the Arduino.** If not running smoothly check the pin outs as different firing order from the other programs. The actual wiring diagram has not changed from the previous 4-wire example.

/* Arduino_AccelStepper_4_Wire_H_Bridge 4/23/2019 Herb Norbom
* single stepper with variable inputs to control speed, position and acceleration
* When powered up where stepper is becomes position 0

Arduino Projects   pg. 71

```
 *  Your moves are in reference to that position 0, multiple moves adjust based on position 0
 *  Enter 0 to return to start or 'h' to reset servo to zero
 *  As setup to test position, speed and acceleration precede each input with p,s,a
 */
#include <AccelStepper.h>
#define HALF4WIRE 8         //using halfstep so 200 steps is 180 degrees
// Motor pin definitions
#define motorPin4  8    // B2
#define motorPin3  9    // B1
#define motorPin1  10   // A1
#define motorPin2  11   // A2

// Initialize with pin sequence 10,11,9,8
AccelStepper stepper_4_wire(HALF4WIRE, motorPin1, motorPin2, motorPin3, motorPin4);

String inputString="";
boolean stringComplete = false;
String temp ="";
int tempI = 0;
float tempF =0.0;
float MaxSpeed=1000.0;
float Acceleration = 700.0;
int Speed = 800;

void setup() {
  Serial.begin(9600);
  Serial.println("For position enter p + integer");
  Serial.print("For maximum speed enter m + integer. Current= ");
  Serial.println(MaxSpeed);
  Serial.print("For Acceleration enter a + float or integer. Current= ");
  Serial.println(Acceleration);
  Serial.print("For Speed enter s + integer. Current= ");
  Serial.println(Speed);
  Serial.println("For two revolutions enter f  ");
  Serial.println("Reset Servo to position 0   enter h  ");
  Serial.println("Ready...");

  inputString.reserve(20);
  stepper_4_wire.setMaxSpeed(MaxSpeed);    //default 1000.0, 10 very slow to 1000 can be integer
  stepper_4_wire.setAcceleration(Acceleration); //default  700.0
  stepper_4_wire.setSpeed(Speed);        //default 800 doesn't appear to work with this stepper
}

void loop() {
  if (stringComplete){
```

```
Serial.print("Starting Position: ");
Serial.println(stepper_4_wire.currentPosition());
Serial.print("Value entered: ");
Serial.println(inputString);

int len = inputString.length();
if (inputString[0] == 'p'){        //move to position
  for (int x =1;x <len;x++){
    temp = temp+ inputString[x];
  }
  tempI = temp.toInt();
  stepper_4_wire.moveTo(tempI);
}
if (inputString[0] == 'm'){        //set maxmium speed
  for (int x =1;x <len;x++){
    temp = temp+ inputString[x];
  }
  tempF = temp.toFloat();
  MaxSpeed = tempF;
  stepper_4_wire.setMaxSpeed(MaxSpeed);
}
if (inputString[0] == 'a'){        //set Acceleration
  for (int x =1;x <len;x++){
    temp = temp+ inputString[x];
  }
  tempF = temp.toFloat();
  Acceleration = tempF;
  stepper_4_wire.setAcceleration(Acceleration);
}
if (inputString[0] == 's'){        //set Speed
  for (int x =1;x <len;x++){
    temp = temp+ inputString[x];
  }
  tempI = temp.toInt();
  Speed = tempI;
  stepper_4_wire.setSpeed(Speed);
  Serial.print("Starting Speed: ");
  Serial.println(stepper_4_wire.speed());
}
if (inputString[0] == 'f'){        //forward two revolutions
  stepper_4_wire.moveTo(800);
}
if (inputString[0] == 'h'){        //reset servo to position 0
  stepper_4_wire.setCurrentPosition(0);
}
```

```
      inputString="";
      stringComplete = false;
      tempF = 0.0;
      temp="";
      tempI = 0;
    }
  stepper_4_wire.run();  // stepper moves based on input
}


void serialEvent() {
  while (Serial.available()) {
    char inChar = (char)Serial.read();     // get the new byte
    inputString += inChar;              // add it to the inputString
    if (inChar == '\n') {
      stringComplete = true;
    }
  }
}
```

Project 28 MPU6050

We look at this project as an introduction to the MPU6050 sensor by InvenSense. This motion sensor has extensive capabilities and the purpose of this project is to give you ideas on how to work with it. There are numerous information sources on the internet. Your first step needs to be obtaining the datasheet and Register Map. One source is InvenSense. https://www.invensense.com/wp-content/uploads/2015/02/MPU-6000-Datasheet1.pdf and https://www.invensense.com/wp-content/uploads/2015/02/MPU-6000-Register-Map1.pdf

A nice source of general information can be found at https://www.invensense.com/wp-content/uploads/2015/02/MPU-6000-Register-Map1.pdf.

Our sample program does require you to have the "Wire library". https://www.arduino.cc/en/reference/wire


```
/*Arduino_MPU6050_pitch_roll_yaw   Herb Norbom 11/10/19
   MPU-6050, raw values, and calculated roll, pitch and yaw displayed on serial monitor
   Roll is rotation about the x axis (-180 to 180 deg)
   Pitch is the rotation about the y axis (-90 to 90 deg)
   Yaw is the rotation about the z axis (-180 to 180 deg)
*/
#include<Wire.h>
const int MPU6050_Address=0x68;
long accelX, accelY, accelZ, temp, gyroX, gyroY, gyroZ;
long pitch, roll, yaw;
long mag_x, mag_y;
```

```
void setup(){
 Wire.begin();
 Wire.beginTransmission(MPU6050_Address);
 Wire.write(0x6B); Wire.write(0);          // a wakeup
 Wire.endTransmission(true);
 Serial.begin(9600);
 }
void loop(){
 Wire.beginTransmission(MPU6050_Address);
 Wire.write(0x3B);                   //register to begin reads with ACCEL_XOUT_H
 Wire.endTransmission(false);
 Wire.requestFrom(MPU6050_Address,14,true); //read 14 register, each register 8 bit
 accelX=Wire.read()<<8|Wire.read();       // two registers to get one 16 bit value
 accelY=Wire.read()<<8|Wire.read();
 accelZ=Wire.read()<<8|Wire.read();
 temp=Wire.read()<<8|Wire.read();   //while not used left in for ease of reading registers
 gyroX=Wire.read()<<8|Wire.read();
 gyroY=Wire.read()<<8|Wire.read();
 gyroZ==Wire.read()<<8|Wire.read();
 Serial.print("RawX= \t"); Serial.print(accelX);
 Serial.print("\tRawY= \t"); Serial.print(accelY);
 Serial.print("\tRawZ= \t"); Serial.println(accelZ);

 pitch = 180 * atan2(accelX, sqrt(accelY*accelY + accelZ*accelZ))/PI;
 roll = 180 * atan2(accelY, sqrt(accelX*accelX + accelZ*accelZ))/PI;
 mag_x = gyroX*cos(pitch) + gyroY*sin(roll)*sin(pitch) + gyroZ*cos(roll)*sin(pitch);
 mag_y = gyroY*cos(roll) - gyroZ*sin(roll);
 yaw = 180 * atan2(-mag_y,mag_x)/PI;
 Serial.print("pitch= \t"); Serial.print(pitch);
 Serial.print("\troll= \t"); Serial.print(roll);
 Serial.print("\tyaw= \t"); Serial.println(yaw);
 Serial.println();
 delay(500); }
```

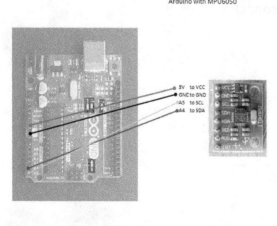

Arduino with MPU6050

5V   to VCC
GND to GND
A5 to SCL
A4 to SDA

C:\Users\Herb\Documents\BOOKSpublish\Arduino Projects\[ArduinoProjects.xlsx]MPU6050_Wiring

COM9				— □ ×
				Send
pitch= 3	roll=	43	yaw=	20
RawX= 904	RawY=	11188	RawZ=	11840
pitch= 3	roll=	43	yaw=	20
RawX= 812	RawY=	11224	RawZ=	11704
pitch= 2	roll=	43	yaw=	-126
RawX= 900	RawY=	11208	RawZ=	11772
pitch= 3	roll=	43	yaw=	8
RawX= 836	RawY=	11088	RawZ=	11712
pitch= 2	roll=	43	yaw=	-140
RawX= 844	RawY=	11108	RawZ=	11772
pitch= 2	roll=	43	yaw=	-155

☑ Autoscroll ☐ Show timestamp   Both NL & CR ⌄   9600 baud ⌄   Clear output

Before we get into this you need to know that while the Bluetooth module is active you **can not** upload a program to the Nano. When we need to upload, we just disconnect the power VCC jumper wire between the Nano and the Bluetooth. (You can leave the USB connection to the Arduino on if desired.)

```
/*NanotwoServoBluetooth  Herb Norbom 11/3/2019 using micro servos continuous rotation
 *Using Bluetooth
*/
#include <Servo.h>
Servo myservoLT;  // create servo object to control LEFT servo
Servo myservoRT;  // create servo object to control RIGHT servo

#define startLt 13     // LED flash light on board the Nano
char inChar =0;        // for serial input
int speedRT = 90;      //center position is 90. Used different values to balance servos
int speedLT = 95;      //center positions off from 90
int speedFact =30;     //for setting speed
#define leftServo 3     // LEFT Servo
#define rightServo 9    //RIGHT Servo
      //servo 90 stop, top 180, bottom 0
void setup() {
  Serial.begin(9600);
  Serial.println("Starting...");
  Serial.print(speedLT);
  Serial.print(", ");
  Serial.println(speedRT);
  FlashLED();
  delay(2000); //Pause approx 2 seconds (2000 milliseconds)
}

void loop(){
  if ( Serial.available()>0){
   inChar = Serial.read();
   Serial.println(inChar);
   if (inChar == '2')
      {stRev();}
   else if (inChar == '5')  //stop
```

```
        {allStop();}
      else if (inChar == '8')   //forward
        {stFwd();}
      else if (inChar == '4')   //turn Left
        {tLeft();}
      else if (inChar == '6')   //turn Right
        {tRight();}
      else if (inChar == '9')     //half right turn
       {halfRight();}
      else if (inChar == '7')     //half left turn
       {halfLeft();}
    }
}


void allStop(){
  myservoLT.write(speedLT);
  myservoRT.write(speedRT);
  myservoLT.detach(); //detach servo to prevent "creeping" effect
  myservoRT.detach(); //detach servo to prevent "creeping" effect
}
void tLeft(){
  myservoLT.attach(leftServo);  // attach the servo on pin leftServo to the LEFT servo
  myservoLT.write((speedLT-speedFact)); //counterclockwise rotation was 0
  myservoRT.attach(rightServo);
  myservoRT.write((speedRT-speedFact)); //clockwise rotation was 180
  delay(700);
  allStop();
}
void halfLeft(){
  myservoLT.attach(leftServo);
  myservoLT.write((speedLT-speedFact));
  myservoRT.attach(rightServo);
  myservoRT.write((speedRT-speedFact));
  delay(250);
  allStop();
}
void tRight(){
  myservoLT.attach(leftServo);
```

```
  myservoLT.write((speedLT+speedFact));
  myservoRT.attach(rightServo);
  myservoRT.write((speedRT+speedFact));
  delay(700);
  allStop();
}
void halfRight(){
  myservoLT.attach(leftServo);
  myservoLT.write((speedLT+speedFact));
  myservoRT.attach(rightServo);
  myservoRT.write((speedRT+speedFact));
  delay(250);
  allStop();
}
void stFwd(){
  myservoLT.attach(leftServo);
  myservoLT.write((speedLT-speedFact));
  myservoRT.attach(rightServo);
  myservoRT.write((speedRT+speedFact));
  delay(1000);
  allStop();
}
void stRev(){
  myservoLT.attach(leftServo);
  myservoLT.write((speedLT+speedFact));
  myservoRT.attach(rightServo);
  myservoRT.write((speedRT-speedFact));
  delay(500);
  allStop();
}

void FlashLED(){
  digitalWrite(startLt, HIGH);
  delay(5);
  digitalWrite(startLt, LOW);
}
```

The wiring for the Arduino Bluetooth is as follows. This diagram shows the servos also.

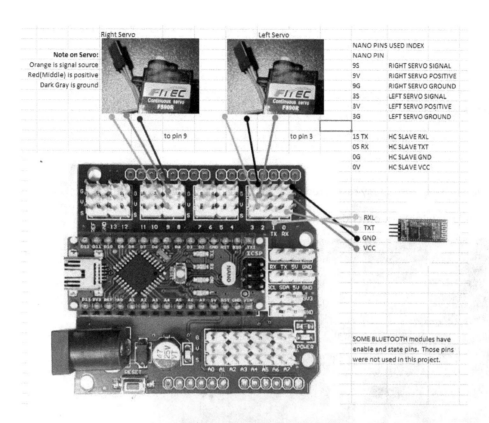

NANO PINS USED INDEX	
NANO PIN	
9S	RIGHT SERVO SIGNAL
9V	RIGHT SERVO POSITIVE
9G	RIGHT SERVO GROUND
3S	LEFT SERVO SIGNAL
3V	LEFT SERVO POSITIVE
3G	LEFT SERVO GROUND
1S TX	HC SLAVE RXL
0S RX	HC SLAVE TXT
0G	HC SLAVE GND
0V	HC SLAVE VCC

Note on Servo:
Orange is signal source
Red(Middle) is positive
Dark Gray is ground

Right Servo — to pin 9

Left Servo — to pin 3

RXL
TXT
GND
VCC

SOME BLUETOOTH modules have enable and state pins. Those pins were not used in this project.

On our PC we are running Windows10, other versions of Windows should work. Of course, your PC must have Bluetooth.

Find the Bluetooth & other devices screen. As shown in the following my Arduino Bluetooth is not connected. Before you can add a device make sure that Bluetooth is 'On'.

Power on the Bluetooth module. In my case a red LED will be flashing on the Bluetooth.

On the PC select "Add Bluetooth or other device".

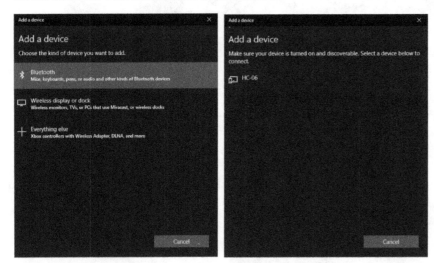

Select Bluetooth. After a brief search your Bluetooth should be shown, mine is HC-06.

Select the device and enter the PIN for your device. Usually 1234 or 0000 and select 'Connect'.

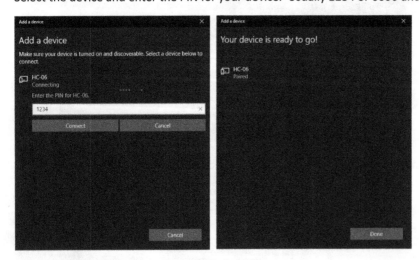

Sometimes you need to try the connect twice. But when successful you will see the paired message.

Disconnect the USB cable and power the Nano from an external power source. Testing with software called PuTTY.
See the Appendix for information on obtaining the free software. Use Device Manager to determine appropriate
com port.

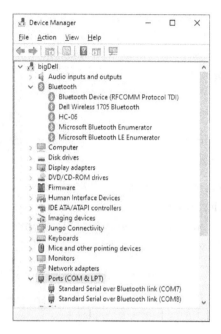

Depending on timing of the power up you may need to press the reset button on the Arduino or shield to get the
startup message.

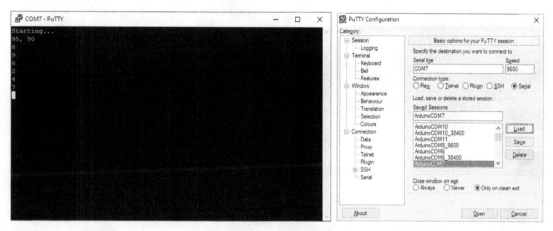

The way I have PuTTY setup I do not need to press 'Enter' with each keypad entry.

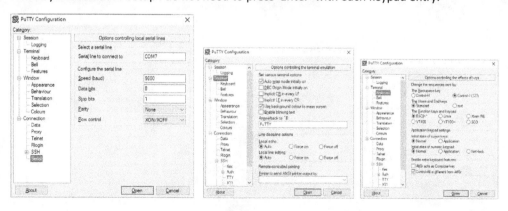

Arduino Projects

MIT App Inventor-Setup

This software is slick. We are not going to do a full tutorial as there are very good ones on the web. In any event you will need to download the software to your PC. You will develop the application on your PC and then you can quickly port it or upload it to your Android Smartphone. For this project we are using a Samsung Galaxy S9+. The web site http://appinventor.mit.edu/explore/about-us.html has tutorials. We sign in with our Google account. Note, your projects are stored in the cloud.

The free software for Windows is available for free at http://appinventor.mit.edu/explore/ai2/windows.html. There is a Mac OS X installation available at http://appinventor.mit.edu/explore/content/mac.html.

The information shown is for a Windows installation. The software you will need to download is approximately 80Mb. Visit the web site for complete instructions. I did install the emulator also. The emulator is good, but it does not handle Bluetooth blocks. Tends to hang when running with a Bluetooth command. The emulator is very handy for visualizing how the application will look on the Android device.

Before building our application please do some of the tutorials, that will make life a little less frustrating.

On our Android device the Developer Option needed to be turned on. For Samsung this link maybe of use. https://www.samsung.com/uk/support/mobile-devices/how-do-i-turn-on-the-developer-options-menu-on-my-samsung-galaxy-device/

You will also need to install the "mit ai2 companion" on your Android device. It is available on the play store.

MIT App with Bluetooth

The following screen shots show the project. This is to connect to the Nano two servo Bluetooth project

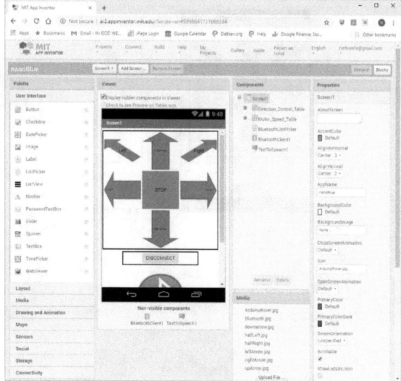

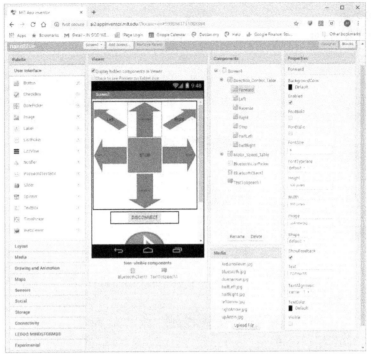

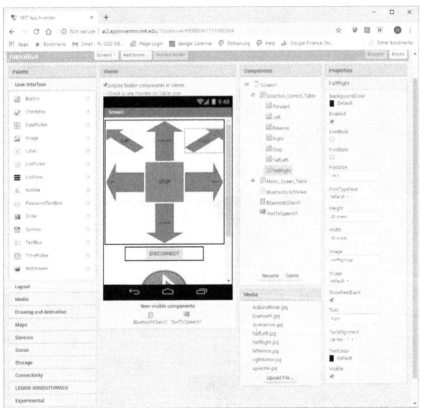

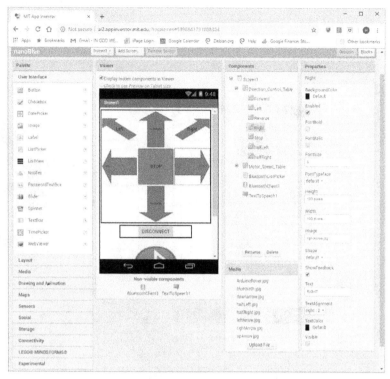

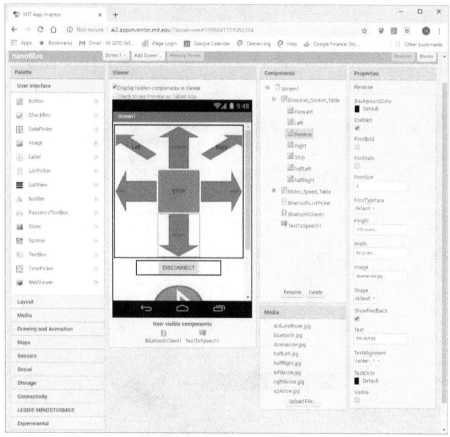

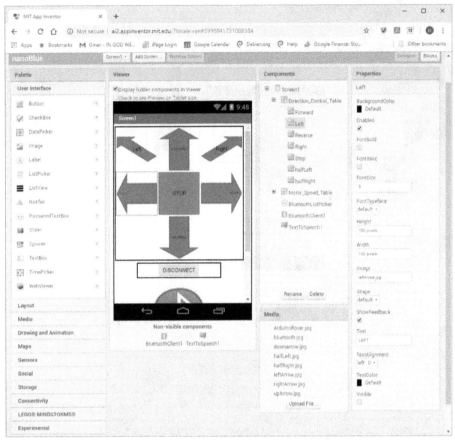

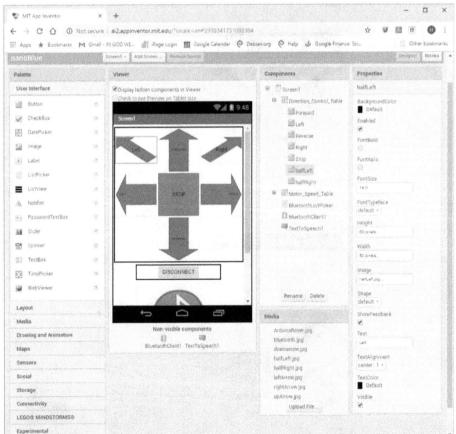

Arduino Projects

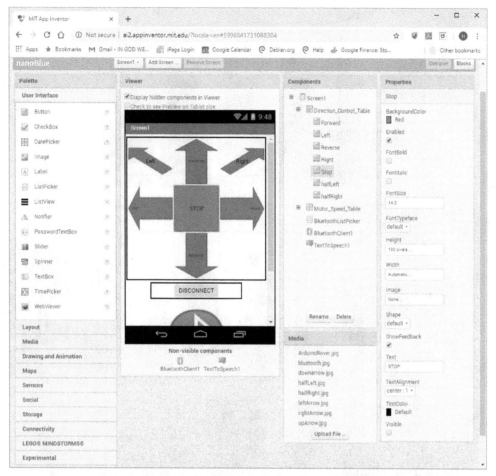

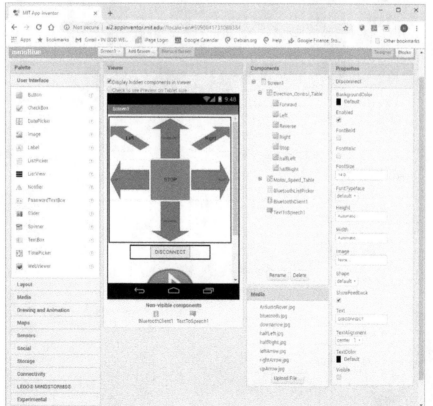

Arduino Projects

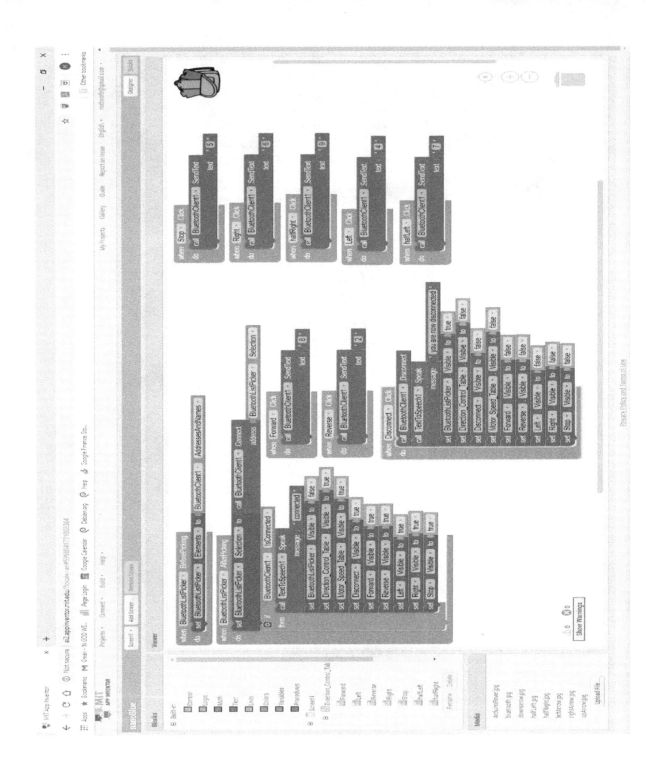

Arduino Projects

Like any program there are numerous methods to achieve the goal. Once installed and running when you click on the Bluetooth icon and connect a voice will announce "connected". When you select disconnect a voice will announce "you are disconnected".

When you are ready to try your application on your Android. Select "Build" and App (provide QR code for .apk). This generates or builds the program. After the program is built a "QR Code" is displayed. Open the "mit ai2 companion" on your Android and select "scan QR code". Your Android device will scan the code and load the program.

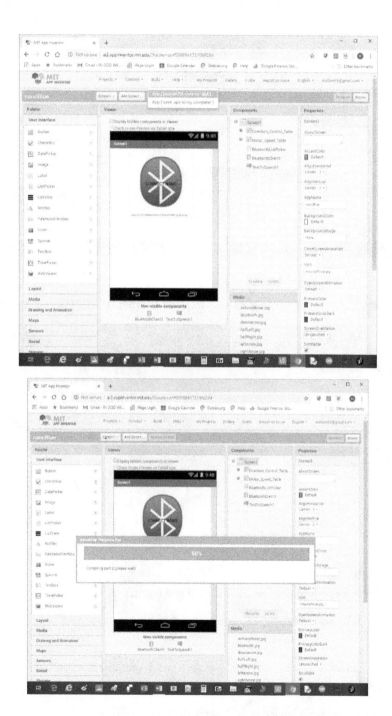

Start the MIT AI2 Companion and select 'scan QR code', aim your Android at the PC screen and the

Open from the installer or find your program on the Android and run it.

If you were connected and the program abended. You may not be able to reconnect until you power down the Arduino and Bluetooth.

If the Bluetooth list picker cannot find your Arduino Bluetooth check that the Bluetooth is wired correctly, powered and that the Android device is paired with the Bluetooth module.

Check under 'settings' on your Android device have Bluetooth "on".

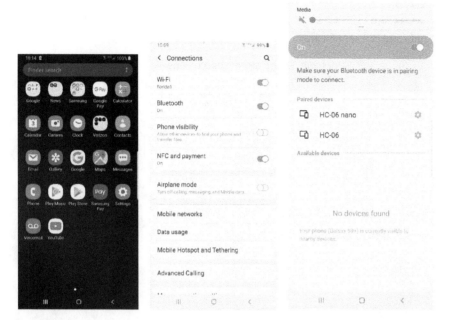

The finished Nano Bluetooth Robot is not a handsome fellow. We are sure you will do better.

Now that you have your Bluetooth Nano running you will probably want to improve the program. For starters we noticed that with a fully charged battery the turns are running too long. Suggest setting the delay lower. Also, if not going in a straight line adjust the motor speedRT and/or speedLT settings in your Arduino script.

Startup sends left and right motor speeds and distance inches.

Pressing 's' and servo search runs

Press 'a' three times and you see the speed of the right motor increases.

Try the other commands and with the motors powered your robot should move. Be careful that it does not run off your table.

Try the commands from the PuTTY software, you can use the existing Com link or try with the Bluetooth module. Review the Nano section if having problems.

Project 30 RFM69HCW

You will need two Nano's which are shown in the examples or two Uno's. One of the problems we encountered was having enough voltage/amperage to maintain the circuit when transmitting or receiving. We found that inserting a capacitor in the circuit eliminated the problem. Auxiliary battery power is also recommended. The programs for transmitting and receiving are the same with some minor changes we added. To transmit and receive you can use the Arduino Serial Monitor for one Nano program and PuTTy for the second Nano. When you are using Arduino IDE be aware that while you can have both programs open but only ONE port can be used at a time for uploading or using the IDE Serial Monitor. We also recommend that you use a Logic Voltage Converter. Two wiring diagrams are shown one with the Logic Voltage Converter and one without. Be aware that the RMF69HCW can be damaged when using 5V.

We purchased the RFM69 Breakout (915MHz) from Sparkfun.
https://www.sparkfun.com/products/12775?_ga=2.207581328.2094783881.1573914706-520796463.1562080459

Sparkfun has put together a very nice Hookup Guide. https://learn.sparkfun.com/tutorials/rfm69hcw-hookup-guide#hardware-connections. The two programs are based on the Sparkfun example with minor changes. The RFM69 library will need to be installed.

In our example we used the 3.3V Arduino pin to power the breadboard and the RFM69HCW. The antenna size is critical. With the capacitor in place we did not need an external power supply in addition to the USB. You will need to set up two Nano's with breadboards and RFM69HCW radio modules.

```
// Arduino_RFM69HCW_master 11/16/2019
// RFM69HCW Example Sketch
// Send serial input characters from one RFM69 node to another
// Based on RFM69 library sample code by Felix Rusu
// http://LowPowerLab.com/contact
// Modified for RFM69HCW by Mike Grusin, 4/16
// This sketch will show you the basics of using an
// RFM69HCW radio module. SparkFun's part numbers are:
// 915MHz: https://www.sparkfun.com/products/12775
// 434MHz: https://www.sparkfun.com/products/12823
// See the hook-up guide for wiring instructions:
// https://learn.sparkfun.com/tutorials/rfm69hcw-hookup-guide
// Uses the RFM69 library by Felix Rusu, LowPowerLab.com
// Original library: https://www.github.com/lowpowerlab/rfm69
// SparkFun repository: https://github.com/sparkfun/RFM69HCW_Breakout
// Include the RFM69 and SPI libraries:
#include <RFM69.h>
#include <SPI.h>

// Addresses for this node. CHANGE THESE FOR EACH NODE!
```

```
#define NETWORKID    0   // Must be the same for all nodes (0 to 255)
#define MYNODEID     1   // My node ID (0 to 255)
#define TONODEID     2   // Destination node ID (0 to 254, 255 = broadcast)

// RFM69 frequency, uncomment the frequency of your module:
//#define FREQUENCY   RF69_433MHZ
#define FREQUENCY     RF69_915MHZ

// AES encryption (or not):
#define ENCRYPT     false // Set to "true" to use encryption
#define ENCRYPTKEY   "TOPSECRETPASSWRD" // Use the same 16-byte key on all nodes

// Use ACKnowledge when sending messages (or not):
#define USEACK      true // Request ACKs or not

// Packet sent/received indicator LED (optional):
#define LED        9 // LED positive pin
#define GND         8 // LED ground pin
#define BASEPRW     30

// Create a library object for our RFM69HCW module:
RFM69 radio;

void setup()
{
  // Open a serial port so we can send keystrokes to the module:
  Serial.begin(115200);
  delay(500);
  char buff[50];
  sprintf(buff, "\nTransmitting at %d Mhz...", FREQUENCY==RF69_433MHZ ? 433 :
FREQUENCY==RF69_868MHZ ? 868 : 915);
  Serial.println(buff);
  Serial.print("Node ");
  Serial.print(MYNODEID,DEC);
  Serial.println(" Master ready");

  // Set up the indicator LED (optional):
  pinMode(LED,OUTPUT);
```

```
  digitalWrite(LED,LOW);
  pinMode(GND,OUTPUT);
  digitalWrite(GND,LOW);

  // Initialize the RFM69HCW:
  //  radio.setCS(10);  //uncomment if using Pro Micro
  radio.initialize(FREQUENCY, MYNODEID, NETWORKID);
  radio.setHighPower(); // Always use this for RFM69HCW
  radio.setPowerLevel(BASEPRW); // power output ranges from 0 (5dBm) to 31 (20dBm)
  // Turn on encryption if desired:
  if (ENCRYPT)
    radio.encrypt(ENCRYPTKEY);
}


void loop()
{
  /* Set up a "buffer" for characters that we'll send:
   SENDING gather serial characters and send them to the other node
   if we (1) get a carriage return, or (2) the buffer is full (61 characters).
   If there is any serial input, add it to the buffer:
  */
  static char sendbuffer[62];
  static int sendlength = 0;
  if (Serial.available()>0)
  {
    char input = Serial.read();
    if (input != '\r') // not a carriage return
    {
      sendbuffer[sendlength] = input;
      sendlength++;
    }
    // If the input is a carriage return, or the buffer is full:
    if ((input == '\r') || (sendlength == 61)) // CR or buffer full
    {
      // Send the packet!
      Serial.print("sending to node ");
      Serial.print(TONODEID, DEC);
      Serial.print(": [");
```

```
    for (byte i = 0; i < sendlength; i++)
      Serial.print(sendbuffer[i]);
      Serial.println("]");

    // There are two ways to send packets. If you want
    // acknowledgements, use sendWithRetry():
    if (USEACK)
    {
      if (radio.sendWithRetry(TONODEID, sendbuffer, sendlength))
        Serial.println("ACK received!");
      else
        Serial.println("no ACK received :(");
    }
    // If you don't need acknowledgements, just use send():
    else // don't use ACK
    {
      radio.send(TONODEID, sendbuffer, sendlength);
    }
    sendlength = 0; // reset the packet
    Blink(LED,10);
  }
}

/* RECEIVING
  In this section, we'll check with the RFM69HCW to see
  if it has received any packets:
*/
  if (radio.receiveDone()) // Got one!
  {
    // Print out the information:
    Serial.print("received from node ");
    Serial.print(radio.SENDERID, DEC);
    Serial.print(": [");

    // The actual message is contained in the DATA array,
    // and is DATALEN bytes in size:
    for (byte i = 0; i < radio.DATALEN; i++)
      Serial.print((char)radio.DATA[i]);
```

```
    Serial.print("], RSSI ");    // RSSI is the "Receive Signal Strength Indicator",
    Serial.println(radio.RSSI); // smaller numbers mean higher power.

    // Send an ACK if requested.
    // (You don't need this code if you're not using ACKs.)
    if (radio.ACKRequested())
    {
      radio.sendACK();
      Serial.println("ACK sent");
    }
    Blink(LED,10);  //visual method of letting you know
  }
}


void Blink(byte PIN, int DELAY_MS)
// Blink an LED for a given number of ms
{
  Serial.println("At blink");
  digitalWrite(PIN,HIGH);
  delay(DELAY_MS);
  digitalWrite(PIN,LOW);
}




// Arduino_RFM69HCW_slave  11/16/2019
// RFM69HCW Example Sketch
// Send serial input characters from one RFM69 node to another
// Based on RFM69 library sample code by Felix Rusu
// http://LowPowerLab.com/contact
// Modified for RFM69HCW by Mike Grusin, 4/16
// This sketch will show you the basics of using an
// RFM69HCW radio module. SparkFun's part numbers are:
// 915MHz: https://www.sparkfun.com/products/12775
// 434MHz: https://www.sparkfun.com/products/12823
// See the hook-up guide for wiring instructions:
// https://learn.sparkfun.com/tutorials/rfm69hcw-hookup-guide
// Uses the RFM69 library by Felix Rusu, LowPowerLab.com
```

```
// Original library: https://www.github.com/lowpowerlab/rfm69
// SparkFun repository: https://github.com/sparkfun/RFM69HCW_Breakout
// Include the RFM69 and SPI libraries:
#include <RFM69.h>
#include <SPI.h>

// Addresses for this node. CHANGE THESE FOR EACH NODE!
#define NETWORKID    0   // Must be the same for all nodes (0 to 255)
#define MYNODEID     2   // My node ID (0 to 255)
#define TONODEID     1   // Destination node ID (0 to 254, 255 = broadcast)

// RFM69 frequency, uncomment the frequency of your module:
//#define FREQUENCY   RF69_433MHZ
#define FREQUENCY     RF69_915MHZ

// AES encryption (or not):
#define ENCRYPT      false // Set to "true" to use encryption
#define ENCRYPTKEY   "TOPSECRETPASSWRD" // Use the same 16-byte key on all nodes

// Use ACKnowledge when sending messages (or not):
#define USEACK       true // Request ACKs or not

// Packet sent/received indicator LED (optional):
#define LED          9 // LED positive pin
#define GND          8 // LED ground pin
#define BASEPRW      1 // play with this 0 to 31, if too high doesn't always work

// Create a library object for our RFM69HCW module:
RFM69 radio;

void setup()
{
  // Open a serial port so we can send keystrokes to the module:
  Serial.begin(115200);
  delay(500);
  char buff[50];
  sprintf(buff, "\nTransmitting at %d Mhz...", FREQUENCY==RF69_433MHZ ? 433 :
FREQUENCY==RF69_868MHZ ? 868 : 915);
```

```
      Serial.println(buff);
      Serial.print("Node ");
      Serial.print(MYNODEID,DEC);
      Serial.println(" SLAVE ready");

      // Set up the indicator LED (optional):
      pinMode(LED,OUTPUT);
      digitalWrite(LED,LOW);
      pinMode(GND,OUTPUT);
      digitalWrite(GND,LOW);

      // Initialize the RFM69HCW:
      // radio.setCS(10);  //uncomment if using Pro Micro
      radio.initialize(FREQUENCY, MYNODEID, NETWORKID);
      radio.setHighPower(); // Always use this for RFM69HCW
      radio.setPowerLevel(BASEPRW); // power output ranges from 0 (5dBm) to 31 (20dBm)
      // Turn on encryption if desired:
      if (ENCRYPT)
        radio.encrypt(ENCRYPTKEY);
    }


void loop()
{
  /* Set up a "buffer" for characters that we'll send:
   SENDING gather serial characters and send them to the other node
   if we (1) get a carriage return, or (2) the buffer is full (61 characters).
   If there is any serial input, add it to the buffer:
  */
  static char sendbuffer[62];
  static int sendlength = 0;
  if (Serial.available() > 0)
  {
    char input = Serial.read();
    if (input != '\r') // not a carriage return
    {
      sendbuffer[sendlength] = input;
      sendlength++;
    }
```

```
  // If the input is a carriage return, or the buffer is full:
  if ((input == '\r') || (sendlength == 61)) // CR or buffer full
  {
    // Send the packet!
    Serial.print("sending to node ");
    Serial.print(TONODEID, DEC);
    Serial.print(": [");
    for (byte i = 0; i < sendlength; i++)
      Serial.print(sendbuffer[i]);
    Serial.println("]");

    // There are two ways to send packets. If you want
    // acknowledgements, use sendWithRetry():
    if (USEACK)
    {
      if (radio.sendWithRetry(TONODEID, sendbuffer, sendlength))
        Serial.println("ACK received!");
      else
        Serial.println("no ACK received :(");
    }
    // If you don't need acknowledgements, just use send():
    else // don't use ACK
    {
      radio.send(TONODEID, sendbuffer, sendlength);
    }
    sendlength = 0; // reset the packet
    Blink(LED,10);
  }
}

/* RECEIVING
  In this section, we'll check with the RFM69HCW to see
  if it has received any packets:
*/
  if (radio.receiveDone()) // Got one!
  {
    // Print out the information:
    Serial.print("received from node ");
```

```
  Serial.print(radio.SENDERID, DEC);
  Serial.print(": [");

  // The actual message is contained in the DATA array,
  // and is DATALEN bytes in size:
   for (byte i = 0; i < radio.DATALEN; i++)
    Serial.print((char)radio.DATA[i]);

  Serial.print("], RSSI ");    // RSSI is the "Receive Signal Strength Indicator",
  Serial.println(radio.RSSI);   // smaller numbers mean higher power.

  // Send an ACK if requested.
  // (You don't need this code if you're not using ACKs.)
  if (radio.ACKRequested())
  {
    radio.sendACK();
    Serial.println("ACK sent");
  }
  Blink(LED,10);  //visual method of letting you know
 }
}

void Blink(byte PIN, int DELAY_MS)
// Blink an LED for a given number of ms
{
 Serial.println("At blink");
 digitalWrite(PIN,HIGH);
 delay(DELAY_MS);
 digitalWrite(PIN,LOW);
}
```

Arduino Nano with RFM69HCW

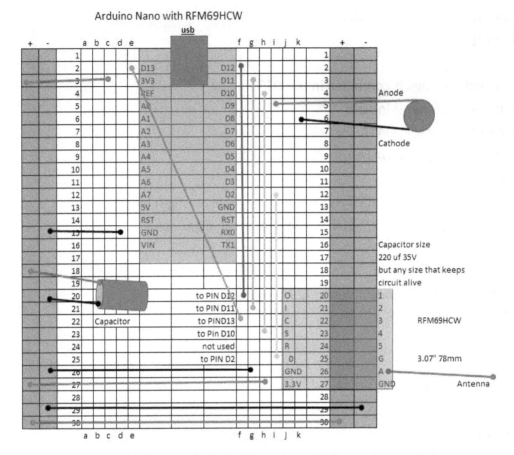

C:\Users\Herb\Documents\BOOKSpublish\Arduino Projects\[ArduinoProjects.xlsx]RFM69HCW_Wiring

Arduino Nano with RFM69HCW and Logic Level Converter 5V to 3V

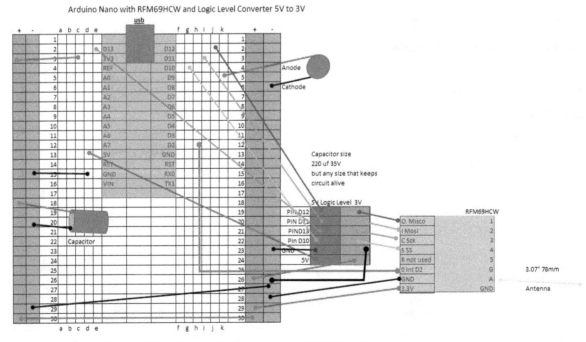

C:\Users\Herb\Documents\BOOKSpublish\Arduino Projects\[ArduinoProjects.xlsx]RFM69HCW_Wiring (2)

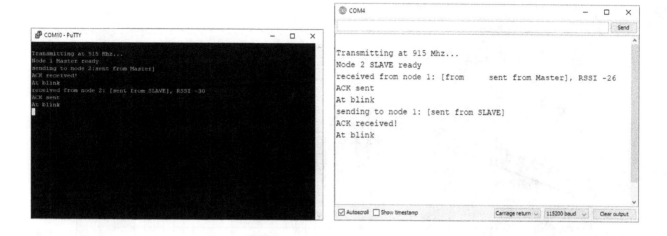

Project 31 GPS coordinate logger

Add a GPS device to two previous projects. With the SD and the OLED you can develop a portable GPS tracker that records positions. Upload the file from the SD to google maps and you can plot your positions. You will need to install TinyGPS++, Software Serial and SD. Wire is also required. Memory on the chip became a problem, hence TinyGPS++. Pin selection also was an issue necessitated using SoftwareSerial. We ended up using the Arduino Nano mounted on a Sensor Shield or expansion board. The Uno could also be used and is show in the wiring diagram. You will need external power beyond what the USB can provide.

We downloaded TinyGPS++ zip file from GitHub
https://github.com/mikalhart/TinyGPSPlus/blob/master/src/TinyGPS%2B%2B.h. **Note:** The Arduino library has TinyGPS available, not sure if it will work as well. Try the example programs included to ensure GPS working.

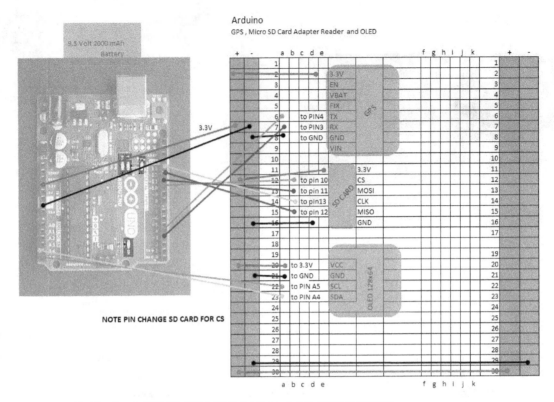

Arduino
GPS , Micro SD Card Adapter Reader and OLED

	+	-		a	b	c	d	e				f	g	h	i	j	k		+	-
1																		1		
2									3.3V									2		
3									EN									3		
4									VBAT									4		
5									FIX									5		
6				to PIN4					TX	GPS								6		
7				to PIN3					RX									7		
8				to GND					GND									8		
9									VIN									9		
10																		10		
11									3.3V									11		
12				to pin 10					CS	SD CARD								12		
13				to pin 11					MOSI									13		
14				to pin13					CLK									14		
15				to pin 12					MISO									15		
16									GND									16		
17																		17		
18																		18		
19																		19		
20				to 3.3V					VCC	OLED 128x64								20		
21				to GND					GND									21		
22				to PIN A5					SCL									22		
23				to PIN A4					SDA									23		
24																		24		
25																		25		
26																		26		
27																		27		
28																		28		
29																		29		
30																		30		

9.5 Volt 2000 mAh Battery

3.3V

NOTE PIN CHANGE SD CARD FOR CS

C:\Users\Herb\Documents\BOOKSpublish\Arduino Projects\[ArduinoProjects.xlsx]GPS_SD Card Wiring

You will also need to install the SSD1306Asci library. Found this necessary to accommodate limited program memory available on chip. As just doing Ascii and no graphics a good trade off.

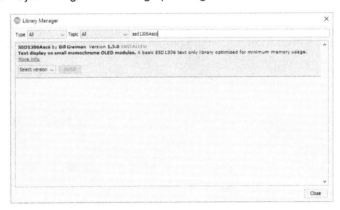

The SoftwareSerial library is included with the Arduino IDE.

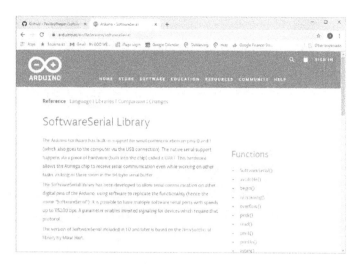

The program shown in the following writes to the SD after 20 reads of GPS, change as you need it. You will probably need a text editor to clean up the Gps log file, remove zero entries.

/* Arduino_GPS_SD_Log_Ascci2   Herb Norbom 11/25/2019

Logs Latitude and Longitude to SD card. Tests if file exists if file exists
will create a new file.
Limit 10 new files. If limit met will add data to last file,myGPSx.CSV'.
Using Adafruit Ultimate GPS, product ID 746, antenna added
Based on TingGPS++ library by Mikal Hart
Using SSD1306Ascii library by Bill Greiman.
If problems with SD not initializing it may be due to low power. Found that
even with USB connected had intermittent problems, with battery connected no
problems. For testing while connected to Serial Monitor various info displayed.
*/

```
#include <TinyGPS++.h>
#include <SoftwareSerial.h>
#include <SD.h>
#include <Wire.h>
#include "SSD1306Ascii.h"
#include "SSD1306AsciiAvrI2c.h"
#define I2C_ADDRESS 0x3C   //60 for OLED
#define RST_PIN -1     // Define proper RST_PIN if required.
SSD1306AsciiAvrI2c oled; //setup the oled

TinyGPSPlus gps;        // The TinyGPS++ object
static const int RXPin = 4, TXPin = 3;
SoftwareSerial ss(RXPin, TXPin);  // serial connection to the GPS device Digital Pins
int fileSeq = 1;       //sequencer to help prevent overwriting a file
```

```
File myFile;
String fileName = "myGPS" + String(fileSeq) + ".csv";
String longitude;
String latitude;
String myAltitude;
int SatNumber;
int myCount = 0;          // limit number of readings from GPS
const int SDWrite = 20;    // write to SD after this number of GPS reads
int SDCounter = 0;         // short counter for number of writes to SD

void setup()
{
  Serial.begin(115200);
  delay(2000);
  Serial.println("Initializing SD card...");
  if (!SD.begin(10)) {                //usingpin Arduino D10 pin
    Serial.println("SD init fail");
    oled.println("SD FAIL");
   while (1);
  }

  int tempCounter = 0;
  while (tempCounter < 10) {
   if (SD.exists(fileName)) {
     fileSeq += 1;
     tempCounter += 1;
     fileName = "myGPS" + String(fileSeq) + ".csv";
   } else {
     Serial.println("File not found create new");
     tempCounter = 11;
   }
  }
  myFile.close();
  myFile = SD.open(fileName, FILE_WRITE);
  if (myFile) {
   Serial.print("file opened: ");
  } else {
   Serial.print("error opening: ");
```

```arduino
  }
  Serial.println(fileName);
  myFile.close();
  delay(2000);
  ss.begin(9600);
#if RST_PIN >= 0
  oled.begin(&Adafruit128x64, I2C_ADDRESS, RST_PIN);
#else // RST_PIN >= 0
  oled.begin(&Adafruit128x64, I2C_ADDRESS); //using this as set to -1
#endif // RST_PIN >= 0
  // Call oled.setI2cClock(frequency) to change from the default frequency.
  oled.clear();
  oled.println(fileName);
  oled.setFont(Adafruit5x7);
  oled.set2X();
  oled.clear();
}

void loop()
{
  while (myCount < 5000) {
    myCount += 1;
    delay(300);        //if this too long it appears to mess up the gps reads
    while (ss.available()) {
      gps.encode(ss.read());
    }
    latitude = String(gps.location.lat(), 5); //limit gps to 5 postion to right of decimal
    longitude = String(gps.location.lng(), 5);
    float temp = (gps.altitude.meters());
    myAltitude = temp * 3.2084; //convert meters to feet
    SatNumber = gps.satellites.value();
    Serial.print("CNT: "); Serial.print(myCount);   //myCount is not written to SD
    Serial.print(" LAT: "); Serial.print(latitude);
    Serial.print(" LON: "); Serial.print(longitude);
    Serial.print(" ALT Meters: "); Serial.print(temp);
    Serial.print(" ALT Feet: "); Serial.print(myAltitude);
    Serial.print(" Sat: "); Serial.println(SatNumber);
    oled.clear();
```

```
oled.println(myCount);
oled.println(latitude);
oled.print(" ");
oled.println(longitude);
oled.print(myAltitude);
SDCounter+=1;
if (SDCounter > SDWrite){
  myFile = SD.open(fileName,FILE_WRITE);
  myFile.print(latitude);   //write to SD
  myFile.print(",");
  myFile.println(longitude);
  myFile.close();          // close the file:
  SDCounter = 0;
 }
 }
}
```

It can take awhile for GPS to acquire satellites, especially if indoors.

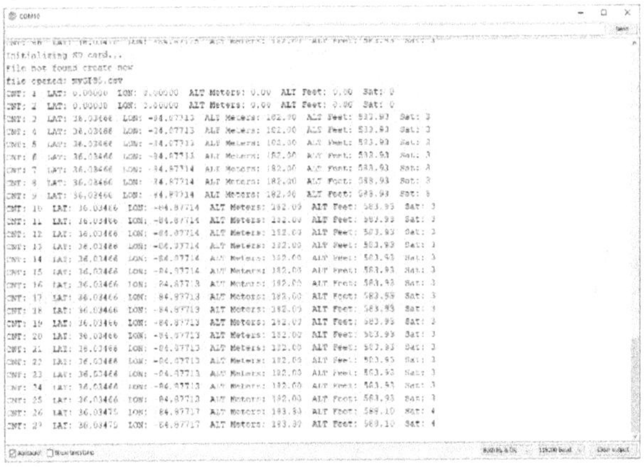

Ran a little test loop to generate two files. Combined them as shown below.

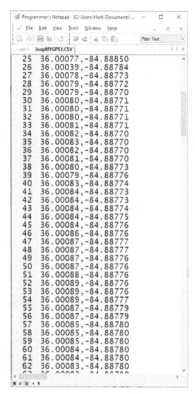

```
25  36.00077,-84.88850
26  36.00039,-84.88784
27  36.00078,-84.88773
28  36.00079,-84.88772
29  36.00079,-84.88770
30  36.00080,-84.88771
31  36.00080,-84.88771
32  36.00080,-84.88771
33  36.00081,-84.88771
34  36.00082,-84.88770
35  36.00083,-84.88770
36  36.00082,-84.88770
37  36.00081,-84.88770
38  36.00080,-84.88773
39  36.00079,-84.88774
40  36.00083,-84.88774
41  36.00084,-84.88773
42  36.00084,-84.88773
43  36.00084,-84.88774
44  36.00084,-84.88775
45  36.00084,-84.88776
46  36.00086,-84.88776
47  36.00087,-84.88777
48  36.00087,-84.88777
49  36.00087,-84.88776
50  36.00087,-84.88776
51  36.00088,-84.88776
52  36.00089,-84.88776
53  36.00089,-84.88776
54  36.00089,-84.88777
55  36.00087,-84.88779
56  36.00087,-84.88779
57  36.00085,-84.88780
58  36.00085,-84.88780
59  36.00085,-84.88780
60  36.00084,-84.88780
61  36.00084,-84.88780
62  36.00083,-84.88780
```

With the combined cvs file we uploaded it to google maps. https://www.google.com/maps/d/
Follow the site directions to upload the file.

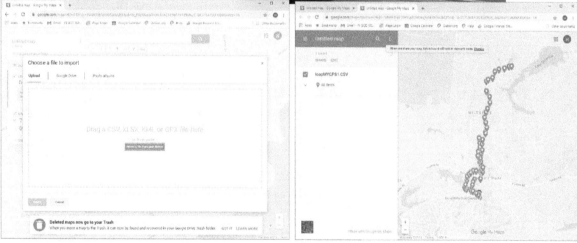

If all goes well, you can produce your trail on the map.

Appendix

PuTTy where to get it

Visit the PuTTy web site at https://www.chiark.greenend.org.uk/~sgtatham/putty/.

Download a stable version, the latest version is 0.70. Choose the appropriate version for your system. We recently downloaded the 0.70 Windows 64-bit version and have had no problems with it. In the book exhibits we were using version 0.63. We have been using various versions of PuTTy for at least ten years.

Additional Information

The digital software source code for the Arduino programs and the MIT App software (.aia) files are available for a limited time and additional fee on the FastSpring Store. https://rymax.onfastspring.com/ While this book does contain the complete printed source code. The code in electronic or digital form is available for a limited time for an additional charge. On the Fast Spring Store web site, the software is listed under the same title as this book. Be sure to use the following discount code "HERB_SAYS_THANKS", this is a limited time special discount 30%. The wiring diagrams are also included in color, which makes them much easier to read. Various pictures of the projects are included.

www.ingramcontent.com/pod-product-compliance
Lightning Source LLC
Chambersburg PA
CBHW080539060326

40690CB00022B/5174